ECOTONE

VOLUME II, NUMBER 1
FALL/WINTER 2006

editor-in-chief
DAVID GESSNER

advisory board
BARBARA BRANNON, MARK COX, PHILIP GERARD,
SARAH MESSER, ROBERT SIEGEL, MICHAEL WHITE

managing editor
JAY VARNER

associate editor
MIRIAM PARKER

editors
LAUREN BREEDEN HODGES, nonfiction
CHRIS MALPASS, poetry
SUMANTH PRABHAKER, fiction
LINDSEY RONFELDT, poetry

designer
SUMANTH PRABHAKER

copyeditors
JENNIFER CARLYLE
HILLARY WENTWORTH
DOUGLASS BOURNE

editorial staff
HANNAH ABRAMS, XHENET ALIU, PAT BJORKLUND,
JENNIFER CARLYLE, DOUGLAS CUTTING, ASHLEY
HUDSON, HILLARY WENTWORTH

founding editors
KIMI FAXON
HEATHER WILSON

Ecotone: reimagining place (ISSN 1553-1775) is published twice yearly by the Department of Creative Writing and the Publishing Laboratory at the University of North Carolina Wilmington. We are grateful for funding from the Landfall Foundation and the UNCW Department of Creative Writing. Subscriptions: $15 (one year, two issues). Single copies and institutional subscriptions are also available.

Please address all correspondence to *Ecotone: reimagining place*, Department of Creative Writing, University of North Carolina Wilmington, 601 South College Road, Wilmington, NC 28403-3297. For submission guidelines, please consult page 169, or visit us online at www.uncw.edu/ecotone.

Copyright © 2006 by the University of North Carolina Wilmington.

On the cover: *The Nature of Things*, 2001, Joan Snyder. Oil, acrylic, herbs, earth, and velvet on canvas, 64″ x 54″. Collection of Andrew Goorno.
On the back: *Beanfield with Music for Molly*, 1984, Joan Snyder. Oil on canvas, 7″ x 9″. Collection of the artist.
Paintings by Joan Snyder appearing on pages 69–76:
All the Things, 2006. Oil, acrylic, fabric, herbs, rosebuds, and pastel on linen, 36″ x 36″.
Late Summer Pond, 2006. Acrylic, paper mache, fabric, and paper on linen, 48″ x 68″.
Alizarin and Ice, 2006. Oil, acrylic, herbs, twigs, seeds, fabric, paper, and glitter on linen, 60″ x 84″.
My Song, 2006. Acrylic, paper mache, herbs, buds, and dried flowers on linen, 36″ x 36″.
Night, 2003. Oil, acrylic, herbs, glitter, and cloth on wood panel, 18″ x 18″.
Baby Blue Yonder, 2006. Acrylic, paper mache, and twigs on linen, 20″ x 24″.
Color/Field, 2005. Acrylic, oil, paper mache, straw, cloth, and seeds on wood panel 40″ x 50″. Collection of Harvey and Phyllis Baumann.
Summer Pond, 2006. Acrylic, paper mache, twigs, straw, paper, and glitter on wood panel, 24″ x 24″.
Joan Snyder is represented by Betty Cuningham Gallery in New York City, Nielsen Gallery in Boston, and Elena Zang Gallery in Woodstock, New York.
All images © Joan Snyder.

ISBN 978-0-9791403-0-3
Ecotone design by Sumanth Prabhaker
Printed in U.S.A. at Thomson-Shore, Inc., Dexter, Michigan

UNCW
CREATIVE WRITING

ecotone \ē'kə-tōn'\ n:

a transitional zone between two communities, containing the characteristic species of each; a place of danger or opportunity; a testing ground.

eco Greek oik-os, house, dwelling + *tone* tonos, tension.

WE ARE GRATEFUL FOR SUPPORT
FROM THE FOLLOWING DONORS:

JOAN H. GILLINGS
FOUNDING BENEFACTOR

DIANE BRANN
BENEFACTOR

JOIN THE FRIENDS OF *Ecotone*

$5000   **FOUNDING BENEFACTOR**
Lifetime subscription

$2000   **BENEFACTOR**
Five-year subscription

$1000   **PATRON**
Three-year subscription

$500   **SPONSOR**
Two-year subscription

$200   **FRIEND**
One-year subscription

DONATIONS ARE TAX-DEDUCTIBLE.

Contents

FROM THE EDITOR   Home and Away   vii

creative nonfiction

BRIAN DOYLE	Fishering	1
MICHAEL P. BRANCH	Endlessly Rocking	20
KATIE FALLON	Ghosts in the Woodshed	77
GARY FINCKE	The Handmade Court	86
SARAH GORHAM	The Edge Effect	99
LIA PURPURA	The Space Between	114
JULIANNA BAGGOTT	Who Needs Nature?	136
JILL TALBOT	Driving I-15	147
J. D. OLENSLAGER	Southern Utah Storms	153
CAROLINE VAN HEMERT	Patterned	154

fiction

JILL MCCORKLE	D-Day	6
ROBERT ANTHONY SIEGEL	Verena Swann	8
REBECCA BARRY	Eye. Arm. Leg. Heart.	39
ALICITA RODRÍGUEZ	Imagining Bisbee	119
SETH HARWOOD	Walden	124
SARAH REITH	Naturalist's Notes	149
EVAN MORGAN WILLIAMS	The Archipelago	157

Ecotone: reimagining place

poetry

Peter Makuck	Release	3
	Laughing Gulls	84
Abe Smith	Hark	19
Sarah Blackman	Ghost Lights	38
	Chronicle	112
Reg Saner	Lone Skier in Glacier George	64
	Fiat Lux	66
	Companionable	67
David Scott	Pelicans	85
Christien Gholson	Crows in the Morning, Crows in the Evening	96
Alissa Nutting	Behind the Wall	113
Claudia MonPere	Across the Broad Hills, 1885	121
Patrick Phillips	Squirrel	123
David Wright	Inerrancy	142

maps

| Aimee Bender | three maps | 144 |

the ecotone interview

| with Reg Saner | | 55 |

art

| Joan Snyder | eight paintings | 68 |

notes on contributors

163

Home and Away
From the Editor

I'd like to see a softball game between two factions in American literature: Home versus Away. The Away team, the exiles and movers, would be captained by Kerouac, Hemingway, and Henry James, the Home team by Thoreau, Dickinson, and Faulkner. While the Homers might be more patient at the plate, the Aways would have the edge in sheer aggression and ambition. No doubt Thomas Wolfe, all six foot seven of him, would bat cleanup for the Aways, having both strip-mined his own hometown for material and coined the phrase that defined the split. He would likely, in the style of his squad, swing mightily for the fences.

If these team names—"Home" and "Away"—seem too bland, we can turn to Wallace Stegner for inspiration. Stegner, who, by the way, would be one of the home team's better players, liked to divide Westerners into two camps: "Boomers" and "Stickers." Boomers were those who came to a place, mined and exploited it for anything from uranium to real estate to tourism, and then moved on. Stickers were those who found a place they loved, stayed there, and fought for it for the rest of their lives.

Boomers and Stickers, then. But whom to root for? Judging by sales and readership, Boomers would have a bigger, louder crowd. But the Stickers have always had a loyal, if small, following (kind of like the Minnesota Twins). Stickers' fans tend to romanticize those who go home again, like Wendell Berry returning to his childhood home in Kentucky. As Berry has written, the effort of truly knowing one place "proposes an enormous labor." The results of that labor, whether with Berry in Kentucky or Thoreau in Concord, are often extraordinary, and some of our best writing of place has come from those who have followed through on the radical notion of staying still, of "wedging downward," as Thoreau put it, in one beloved spot. For instance, here is Berry describing what happened to him after he returned to Kentucky and fully committed to his home place: "I began more seriously than ever to learn the names of things—the wild plants and animals, the natural processes, the local places—and to articulate my observations and memories. My language increased and strengthened, and sent my mind into the place like a live root system." The word "settling" is often a negative one in our culture—with its connotations of accepting less and giving up on dreams—but Berry puts the lie to this. In his words, the idea of settling in a place is nothing short of exhilarating.

Since this is a journal of place, it might be assumed that our editors would root wholeheartedly for Berry and the rest of the Stickers. And we do root them on, we do. But immersion in a place is just one way to write, and if immersion has produced some brilliant place writing, then so has exile. Think of Hemingway re-creating Michigan from the distance of Paris, Wolfe imagining Asheville from New York. As with anything else in this sloppy life, there is no formula, and the theme of finding home, which so sparks Wendell Berry, could easily deaden a different writer. There are those who can only put words to a place once they have left it. And there are those who rely on cycles of movement, of leaving and returning, to excite them. For instance, this simple sentence stands out from the backs of Annie Proulx's recent books: "She lives in Wyoming and Newfoundland." Hard to picture without one hell of a straddle. But you can imagine Proulx, who for my money is as fine a contemporary place writer as we have, immersing herself in Newfoundland, absorbing its rhythms before migrating to Wyoming—so utterly different in climate and culture, smell and sky—where, from a distance, she re-creates the other world (while simultaneously immersing in and absorbing the current place). In this way, I suppose, both movement and settling would stimulate the work. So which team does she play for?

The answer is we don't know. Or really care that much. When it comes to writing about place there is no set method, no one way, no orthodoxy. And, thankfully, there are no teams.

What there is instead is a vast range of sloppy possibility. A thousand ways of making the land where we happen to find ourselves, or the land we have left, a part of the stories that we tell.

In past issues I have used this space to briefly describe each and every piece in the issue. As wonderful as our writers are, this process of

From the Editor

doling out mere phrases of praise begins to feel like feeding single fish to trained dolphins. This time I will instead focus on the work of one writer, the poet and essayist Reg Saner, and on a new feature, one we believe is integral to the vision of *Ecotone*.

From our inception, we have celebrated literature that explores metaphoric maps; with this, our third issue, we will begin to publish literal ones. We've asked writers to submit maps of places that are important to them—childhood places, imagined places from their fiction, places that inspire their work. We put no limit on the content; we supply the pen and paper, and they do the rest. Aimee Bender was the first to respond, and the results—one literal, one introspective, and one very speculative—are fascinating.

This issue also features an interview with the poet and essayist Reg Saner, who has become a close friend, as well as a literary model, for me over the last decade. Reg would no doubt play for the Home team since he is generally associated with one region, the American West, and the mountains and deserts of that region have shaped him—or as he puts it, "We become what surrounds us." Of course there is a professional risk in staking a claim on one place: you are suddenly a "regional" writer, as if we didn't all write from where we are. But calling Reg a "Western writer" seems to me only a little less preposterous than calling Thoreau a "Concord writer." In fact he uses his rambles across Western land as an occasion to speculate on what are, quite literally, universal themes. If he is a regional writer, then his region is the cosmos, and he never walks too far without considering the larger issues that afflict and inspire the human animal, while simultaneously, by employing the universe for perspective, revealing just how small those larger issues are. This sounds very lofty, but what roots it directly to earth is Reg's hiking boots (to be specific, his heavy, Swiss-made Mendls). "Fresh air keeps language alive," he has written. And in his case, his brain seems inter-wired with those bulky boots, movement spurring words about larger worlds. It has been one of my delights as a reader to follow him on his rambles.

As it happened, I was taking an actual, not literary, hike with Reg on September 11, 2001. We had a unique perspective on that day, as we looked down on the country from close to 14,000 feet on the peak of Mount Arapahoe. Having led troops in Korea, Reg is that rare combination of poet and (ex-)warrior, and on that day he accurately predicted that after a period of shock the country would experience a rising tide of jingoism. But even he couldn't have anticipated the extreme cynicism with which our leaders would funnel our national anguish and rage. Worse than cynics, of course, are true believers. The type of mind that can only see one thing one way, a way of thinking and being antithetical to Reg Saner's own agile thinking. In much of Reg's work the great enemy is dogmatism and orthodoxy, and his own efforts and exertions in the open air are geared toward keeping his mind open, toward resisting, in A. R. Ammons's words, the "humbling of reality to precept." But if Reg is critical of religions and creeds that offer up "pat answers and no questions," he is also, by his own admission, "incorrigibly religious." Each morning he hikes up the mesa behind his house on Colorado's Front Range to collect dawn, and how can that not be a type of worship? The difference is that, unlike much of what passes for religion today, his is a "mystery religion" where admitting uncertainty is a part of the larger prayer. Not taking a "narrow view of what's sacred," he opens himself to a world so obviously and infinitely larger than ours, that to think we could understand and explain it with pat answers would be laughable.

Ecotone

reimagining place

Volume II, Number 1
Fall/Winter 2006

Fishering
Brian Doyle

In the woods here in Oregon there is a creature that eats squirrels like candy, can kill a pursuing dog in less than a second, and is in the habit of deftly flipping over a porcupine and scooping out the meat as if the prickle-pig were a huge and startled breakfast melon. This riveting creature is the fisher, a member of the mustelid family that includes weasels, otter, mink, badgers, ferrets, marten, and (at the biggest and most ferocious end of the family) wolverine. Sometimes called the pekan or fisher-cat, the fisher can be three feet long (with tail) and can weigh as much as twelve pounds. Despite its stunning speed and agility, it is best known not as an extraordinary athlete of the thick woods and snowfields, but as the bearer of a coat so dense and lustrous that it has been sought eagerly by trappers for thousands of years; this is one reason the fisher is so scarce pretty much everywhere it used to live.

Biologist friends of mine tell me there are only two "significant" populations of fisher in Oregon—one in the Siskiyou Mountains in the southwest, called the Klamath population, and the other in the Cascade Mountains south of Crater Lake, called the Cascade population. All of the rare sightings of fisher in Oregon in recent years have been in these two areas. In the northwest coastal woods where I occasionally wander, biologists tell me firmly, there are no fishers and there have been none for more than fifty years.

I am a guy who wanders around looking for nothing in particular, which is to say everything; in this frame of mind I have seen many things, in many venues urban and suburban and rural, and while ambling in the woods I have seen marten kits and three-legged elk and secret beds of watercress and the subtle dens of foxes. I have found thickets of wild grapevines, and secret jungles of salmonberries, and stands of huckleberries so remote and delicious that it is a moral dilemma as to whether or not I should leave a map behind for my children when the time comes for me to add to the compost of the world.

Ecotone: reimagining place

Suffice it to say that I have been much graced in these woods, but to see a fisher was not a gift I expected. Yet recently I found loose quills on the path and then the late owner of the quills, with his or her conqueror atop the carcass staring at me.

I do not know if the fisher had ever seen a human being before; it evinced none of the usual sensible caution of the wild creature confronted with *homo violencia*, and it showed no inclination whatsoever to retreat from its prize. We stared at each other for a long moment and then I sat down, thinking that a reduction of my height and a gesture of repose might send the signal that I was not dangerous and had no particular interest in porcupine meat. Plus, I remembered that a fisher can slash a throat in less than a second.

Long minutes passed. The fisher fed, cautiously. I heard thrushes and wrens. There were no photographs or recordings, and when the fisher decided to evanesce, I did not make casts of its tracks or claim the former porcupine as evidence of fisherness. I just watched and listened and now I tell you. I don't have any heavy message to share. I was only a witness: where there are no fishers there was a fisher. It was a stunning creature—alert, attentive, accomplished, unafraid. I think maybe there is much where we think there is nothing. Where there are no fishers there was a fisher. Remember that.

— looked up to see what is was.

Release
Peter Makuck

With rod and tackle box,
I'm slogging through soft sand,

a red sun going down in the surf,
swag-belly clouds drifting in

with Ray, only two months dead,
going on about girls that summer

we studied French in Québec and
guzzled Labatts at the *Chien d'Or*,

about how he'll marry again, keep
at it until he gets it right—*Pas vrai?*

Above the tidewrack, a woman
in a two-piece with half my years

kneels in the sand struggling
with a pillow of feathers,

one wing flapping—a pelican
all tangled in fish line, treble hook

in the bill pouch, the other in its wing.
Ray says, *Ask her out for a drink*

but she says, *Could you give me a hand?*
I drop the tackle and secure the wing

Ecotone: reimagining place

while she croons to calm him and
with one free hand untangles the line.

With pliers from the tackle box,
I expose the barbs and carefully clip,

a total of six loud snaps. Then I hold
the bird while she frees the last tangle

and we step back, join the onlookers,
a father explaining care to his kids.

The pelican now tests his wings, rowing
in place. He looks around and seems

to enjoy the attention, just as Ray did
in bars, buying drinks and telling jokes.

But this college boy with a can of Bud
is no joke and says they watched it flap

all afternoon from that deck on the dune.
His buddy agrees with a belch

that buys a round of frat boy laughter.
Ray is saying the kid needs his clock cleaned

when the brownie waddles up
and puts his foot on top of mine.

He tilts his head to catch my look, then
flapping runs into the air, tucks his feet,

and climbs, turning over our small circle,
before heading west. Dazzled and dumb,

I'm faintly aware of the woman, then gone,
weightless and soaring over water, looking

down on myself slogging through sand,
certain that I'm being watched,

if only by another self
who will have to tell how it happened.

D-Day
Jill McCorkle

You have been waiting forever—beached, scorched, weary—white handkerchief in your pocket ready to wave. But the lawyers won't let you quit. They save you from *yourself* even though you want to plead guilty—unhappy in the first degree. When you enlisted and they asked *Do you take?* you thought they said *Do you fake?* And vowed you did—desire, joy, contentment. Survival in the trenches. You just wanted to surrender. Instead you got a surprise attack: a man in uniform with orders for your court appearance and documentation of your entire tour of duty. *Fuck you very much*, you said sweetly, and let loose your big dog. If you owned a firearm you might have loaded it.

And now you are in court. Low rent district—nasty tile floor, old dried flowers and portraits of dead lawyers. No one resembles Matlock. Perry Mason was never here. The wavy glass door marked *Private* looks promising until it swings open to reveal humans stuffed into dress shirts and panty hose. They hold your fate in their sticky hands. You feel a weak wash of security that at least they are not distracted by good health or fashion sense. You are in camouflage; pilled up cardigan, threadbare Keds—*frumpy deprived housewife sprung from domestic dungeon*. Camouflage also protects you from single marksmen as they scope out their next hit. You hiss, cough phlegm, scratch in a way that suggests feminine infections. You carry your rations in a paper sack that rattles when you accidentally drop it—bruised up apple, cheap lipstick, forty-seven cents—*pitiful*. You scoop it up before they take that, too.

Your children—badges of honor—are why you didn't go AWOL years ago. Innocent lives caught in the crossfire; cold bite of reality as they spin on playgrounds, slouch through high school, sink to nearly grown knees in disillusionment and despair. They weep in anger and frustration, fear and sadness—they beg hope for a better future. And that is why you sit here alone in a shitty outfit, stuffing money into the outstretched hands of those who promise to liberate you. You will surrender everything for your children's future. You will eat a bullet, hug a grenade, take a bayonet right through the heart. What you will not do is teach them that it is okay to sacrifice their lives for wars not worth fighting. Why should they live in trenches when beckoned by peaceful shores?

Verena Swann
ROBERT ANTHONY SIEGEL

Dead men are more domineering than living ones, thought Verena Swann. They lecture and direct and give orders, while their widows sit around the circular table, nodding their heads and weeping and promising to stay true to them always.

Verena recognized the situation but accepted it as inevitable. The dead had such pressing needs—to be listened to, to be understood, to be consoled. She herself was much closer to her husband, Theodore, now that he was dead. At his demand, she had learned how to enter into the trance state, to open herself like a door, so that his disembodied spirit could rush into her like water into a bottle. What resulted was an entwining more extreme than marriage can ever be among the living: his hand moved her pen. Her mouth formed his words. She shook with his laughter and cried with his sorrow.

Under his tutelage, she had set herself up as a spirit medium and done extremely well: her sittings were always full, her spirit lectures crowded. But when she closed her eyes to sleep, she would still see the sitters, her patrons, staring at her, their faces fizzling with emotion like glasses of champagne. They wore black dresses and black veils, and lockets and rings containing sacred remnants: curly locks of hair, nail parings. In their handbags they carried photographs and leather gloves and war medals, to pull out and sniff like posies, to put in their mouths and press against their eyes. The sheer physicality of their worship was awful, oppressive. And then she would remember how Theodore used to fit himself to the curve of her body when he was still alive, how he would press his chest against her back and the tops of his thighs against her legs, how one hand would cup her breast.

They had met almost ten years earlier at a Broadway arcade. She had gone with two other girls from the millinery shop to see the dancing chicken, the minstrel show, the carnivorous plant, and to ask questions of the fortune-teller. She noticed him in the shooting gallery, a dashing figure in his dark blue naval uniform, picking off the mechanical ducks one after the other with a little air rifle. She remembered his icy white teeth, his dark eyes, the sea-black of his hair and beard. He introduced himself later in the café, bought her an ice cream, and afterward escorted her through the exhibits. They watched a strange mechanical figure, an automaton, defeat one player after another at chess, and they stopped at a booth where a scientific gentleman displayed a little electromagnetic machine, powered by a hand crank. He told Theodore to hold the wire in his palm and clasp Verena's hand in his. The man cranked, and she felt a strange force shoot through Theodore's hand and into hers, a kind of prickly excitement.

"Now let go," said the man, but neither of them could; their fingers would not move. Their hands were melded together, and they laughed—a little wildly, as if riding a runaway horse.

Three months after they were married, Theodore took ship for the Arctic Circle—a surveying expedition. He came back a year later with sun-blackened skin and a harsh winter gleam in his eyes. "Cold that burns like fire," he told her. "Ice that glows like an incandescent lamp." His attempts to explain only made her realize how little she understood him. Within the year he was gone on another voyage, his absence a ghostly presence in the house, punctuated every three or four months by a thick letter smelling of brine—until a whaler brought news that he had died, with all his party, on an overland trek to the pole. A later ship brought the bodies, packed in polar ice.

Verena had no particular interest in the spirit world. The circles she attended were just a distraction from the boredom of sorrow, a chance to sit among women made drunk by grief; there was some comfort in watching people argue with their dead, though she herself was not so foolish. What was there to say? But then, at Miss Fabricant's, she asked if he missed her and got two sharp raps in return, and her heart started to pound wildly, like a hand beating on a door. The following night, the Warren sisters brought out what they called a planchette, a little heart-shaped board supported by two wheels and a nub of pencil at the narrow end. They placed a sheet of brown butcher's paper beneath it, and then put the tips of their bitten fingers upon the device itself; it skittered from right to left and back again. Afterward, hidden among the scribbling on the paper, they found the letters S-N-O.

Soon Theodore pulled at her day and night, seeking entry into her mind, access to her thoughts, the use of her lips and pen. He was hers in a way he had never been when alive, and yet he was nothing—nothing but the flicker of the candle as she breathed his words.

Living men are no less inscrutable than dead ones, thought Verena, as she watched Mr. Auerbach stir his tea. They glower and brood and fall silent at the oddest times, when a little chat about the weather would suffice. "Some more cookies, Mr. Auerbach?" she asked.

"Thank you, I like the little chocolate ones." He reached and took one from the plate with great delicacy.

Mr. Auerbach was one of her sitters, and something of a favorite. His wheelchair had made her uncomfortable at first, but now seemed a natural extension of his character, which was thoughtful and sensitive. Indeed, his face held such a range and complexity of feeling that she sometimes caught herself staring, as if it were a pond that mirrored the clouds. "Will you be joining us tomorrow?" she asked him, still trying to bridge the silence.

He smiled, as if to point out that he never failed to attend. "Do you ever tire of us, Mrs. Swann? Our tears and fainting spells? Our selfishness?"

Instead of answering she sipped her tea. Where would she be without that selfishness? A widow on a naval pension, forgotten by the world. "Helping others makes me happy," she said finally.

"And yet I can't help wondering if you neglect yourself." He put down his coffee cup and smoothed out the blanket that covered his lap. "Mrs. Swann, would you like to go out on a drive someday?"

She didn't quite understand, but felt her face growing hot. "A drive?"

"Some fresh air would do you good, I think. How would tomorrow morning be?"

Verena spent the rest of the day reminding herself to write to Mr. Auerbach and cancel, but there was an article to finish for one of the spiritualist magazines, and a great stack of business correspondence to answer, and it was late at night when she realized that she had forgotten to write him. She went to her bedroom and sat down on the bed, pondering what to do.

On the wall opposite hung a photograph from Theodore's final expedition. It depicted a vast snow plain, at the center of which stood a group of men pulling a sledge. For all she knew, one of those men could have been Theodore—it was impossible to tell. The men were harnessed like horses and leaned forward into their task with great determination, their legs disappearing into the deep snow. Their tracks could be seen stretching off to the left, a fragile trace obliterated by the picture frame. To the right, nothing but unbroken whiteness.

She had never understood why Theodore wanted that. She had never understood how he could trade her for it. And so maybe she had never understood Theodore. There was a part of him that was blank to her.

She had seen him laid out in the coffin the evening before the funeral, dressed in a white tie, morning coat, and striped pants, the Explorer Club's Order of Von Humboldt—a large gold star—pinned to a red sash strung over his shoulder. A face that is not in motion, not animate, is not a face any longer, just a collection of features. The man in the box was most definitely Theodore, but of course was not Theodore, not *her* Theodore. It was as if the string that held all the beads together had been removed, though the beads were still there. The eyes were closed, the forehead waxy, the strong nose powdered, lips and cheeks painted with rouge. Beard and hair glistened with pomade. There was a heavy scent of perfume, clearly meant to mask the other smell beneath it, of sea wrack or seaweed.

She got up and went over to her desk, opened the drawer and removed another, smaller photograph. This one was definitely of Theodore. It had been taken by a crewmember and was dark and blurry, with some kind of stain or discoloration at the bottom where the plate had been spoiled. It showed Theodore standing on the deck of the ship, a day before the expedition went ashore: bearded, sunburned, thin, the bones showing in his face. A strange look in his eyes, which were focused not on the camera, but on the shoreline beyond the ship's railing. Looking away from her at something she could not see.

This was the photograph Verena used as an aid to trance—not the trances she entered on behalf of the sitters, but the private ones she entered in secret, in her bedroom, at those times of utmost despair when she could not bear to be alone.

Her method was to place herself inside the photograph, as if she too had been present on the deck of the ship, as if she were present at this very moment in the little square of time preserved inside the photograph. She imagined what Theodore would look like if she were standing to his left: the sight of his ear, the shape of his profile, and the bump at the midpoint of his nose. Then his right, the view subtly different. She imagined standing behind him, and suddenly she could see what he saw: a land of blue ice lit by the sun. Then she imagined herself sitting at her desk and looking at the photograph as it had been transformed: her standing next to him on the deck of the ship, the two of them looking out at something the viewer could not see.

She took out paper, dipped pen in ink, and returned to the photograph. She tried to follow Theodore's gaze, directed at a shoreline she could not see.

Theodore would have felt nothing but disdain for a man like Mr. Auerbach. She was painfully aware of that. Her husband's definition of manhood was based on a few simple requirements, all of them physical. For Theodore, the test of manhood was cutting ice blocks in temperatures so cold his beard froze. So cold that exposed skin burnt as if seared with a red hot branding iron, raising big red welts. It was man-hauling a 300-pound supply sledge through chest-high drifts of snow.

The pen began to move, but not in the usual way. Normally, the feeling was empty or hollow: she was a reed, a pipe through which something rushed on its way to somewhere else. But this was different; it moved against, not through her; it was hard, it hurt. She was being dragged like a sledge. She tried to resist, to pull back, but it was impossible. The pen scratched and ripped. *His legs*, it said. *Dead branches*. It was often this way; the paper became a collage of the irregular scraps of language available to him in the spirit world. *Rotten stumps*.

Infirm, she said, choosing the most neutral word she could think of. A poor crippled man, no harm to anyone.

Obscenities, scratched the pen. *Men and women spliced together in that way we once.*

We: the word created an empty space in her chest. She remembered lying beside Theodore in bed, arms and legs tangled; she remembered his weight on top of her, making her solid, a part of the world. I miss your touch, she said.

I reach.

And I keep waiting to feel.

I cant.

My body aches to be held. I'm not an old woman yet.

The pen dipped itself into the inkwell and then clawed its way across the page. Anger was always his substitute for sorrow, but it was worse now that he could break nothing but her feelings. *Flesh*, wrote the pen. *Enemy of spirit.*

You will never lose me, she said.

And then came one of his sudden bursts of eloquence, the words forming quickly, fluidly, without resistance: *imagine having a mouth that cant speak unless pressed to another mouth a hand that cant write unless entwined in another hand nothing but borrowed words to catch the feelings that swirl inside me.*

The flow of words stopped, but she was overcome with an image so vivid that it seemed to be right before her. Her entire head was a window. She looked out on a searing blue sky, so blue it made her dizzy—so blue she could taste it on her tongue, the color of a cold so intense it could not be named. The view was cropped in a peculiar way—in a flash she realized she was looking out of an open tent flap. *Have you ever seen something so blue? I should write a novel about it.*

She thought she felt his hand on her arm, his breath on her neck. Her head was swirling. Dictate it to me, she said.

When I was a little boy. Fingers on her neck pointed her head upward to a new shade of blue. As her vision reeled, she caught a glimpse of windows, gables, rooftops, and finally the sky, flowing like fast-moving water. She was running—or he was, the little boy—with that little-boy abandon, lampposts careening past. A musical vibration moved through him, an ascending chord: laughter. *It was blue like that*, he said.

The laughter spiraled through her, but she felt the opposite, a sadness like wood smoke and fallen leaves. Dictate and I will write it down, she said.

You are it, Verena, the novel I am writing.

With that, her hand was her own once again. She was empty now, exhausted, her eyes almost closed, but she looked over the piece of paper on which she had been writing.

Obscenities.

Men and women spliced together in that way we once.

I reach.

I cant.

All that was left was a series of jagged fragments running down the page. She began to have that strange feeling she sometimes had at these moments, doubting how much was real and how much was in her mind. Was she mad? And yet how to explain the words, the handwriting, the lingering feeling of his breath in her ear?

Living or dead, they require such delicate handling, thought Verena. You can never just say what you mean. Hurt them and they fly to pieces.

She stood on the sidewalk in the bright cool light of morning, wondering how to tell Mr. Auerbach that she could not possibly ride with him. He would think it had something to do with his infirmity, which was not the case at all. It had only to do with her and Theodore, with the fact that she was married to a disincarnate spirit.

The issue was pressing. Mr. Auerbach was smiling down at her from his place in the back of an extremely grand open carriage, drawn by two sleek and muscular black horses. "Jim will help you up," he called down to her.

"Thank you," she said, recognizing that this was her chance to offer her apologies. But she grew flustered and missed her moment, and before she knew it the coachman was helping her up the two high steps, into the carriage, and there was no good way to turn back. She felt the gentle sway of the springs as she settled into the red leather seat, as far as possible from Mr. Auerbach. And yet that was only a few inches. She could smell the scent of his pomade, of his tobacco. "Well," she said, adjusting the folds of her clothing. "How spacious."

It did not help that he was looking at her in that way of his. "What a lovely outfit," he said. "The color in particular."

"Oh, this?" Unsure what to do, she had put aside her usual widow's black and dressed as if she really *were* going on a ride: a pearl gray gown and a white canvas riding coat, topped with a straw hat covered with a silk shawl. "Thank you," she said, feeling the heat enter her face.

"Shall we go?"

She gave a nervous laugh—could not help herself. "To be honest, I'm not sure this is a good idea."

"Jim is an excellent driver, Mrs. Swann."

"What I mean is that my work is paramount. I am dedicated to the spirit world and the good I can do for other people."

He looked at her with his large delicate eyes. "But surely a little fresh air won't hurt?" And with that the carriage jerked into motion.

After returning home, Verena went up to her bedroom to change. She got out her most severe black dress, stripped off the gray one, and then wearing only stays and petticoat, poured some water into the basin and rinsed her face and neck. She could still feel the sunlight hot against her cheeks. The streets had been a beautiful chaos: carriages and wagons vying for right of way, the sidewalks overflowing with people in every sort of costume, the women streaks of color beneath great flowered hats. Mr. Auerbach had kept up a steady stream of conversation, so unlike himself, shouting over the noise of traffic: "Are you comfortable, Mrs. Swann? Would you like a shawl? Look over there and there—the department store windows. Are you enjoying this?" And she had shouted back in excited monosyllables: "Yes! Yes! There! I see!"

She picked up the black dress, held it up, and then set it down, thinking of the séance she had to perform that evening, of the sitters pressed around her, their faces hungry for new forms of grief. Would Theodore make it difficult? His rages could be terrible, the words like a poison burning inside her—and his silences much worse. He had in the past withdrawn from her for weeks at a time, angry over a small slight or an imaginary disloyalty.

Was she not loyal? She did everything she could to hold him close, but he was as ungraspable as air. He was a rush of words followed by unaccountable silences, stories within stories, but always full of omissions. She did not even know the truth of how he died.

Tired suddenly, she lay down on the bed and almost instantly felt the pressure at the back of her neck, the weight constricting her chest. She had no pen, no paper, but it did not seem to matter; the writing was there in her mind, as if she had read it before; all she need do now was remember it.

We spent eight days unable to leave the tent before the weather cleared and I gave the order to turn around. I had to, we were already on half rations, and it was forty days travel back to the nearest supply depot. But I was not disappointed really, though I had to go through the motions with the others. No, I found myself strangely thrilled. We threw away whatever we could not carry: the geologic specimens, the scientific instruments, the charts and logs—everything that had made it a real expedition and not just a boys' adventure. And I emptied my mind too, everything that was extraneous to the job of walking. It was so interesting, Verena, to see what's left when you only keep what you need. The thoughts dwindled down to a handful, incredibly precious—that perfume you wore, you remember which—

Lilac.

Yes, a clean, powdery smell. The house we were renting.

On Eighteenth Street.

You remember the brass knocker on the door, the curious—

Yes, shaped like a clamshell.

With the green residue of polish caught in the ridges. I clung to these things, little bits of the past hidden away in my memory. They told me who I was. And then 300 miles more and I threw those away too, threw them to the wind and they were gone. I didn't need them after all. I knew who I was.

You were my husband, she said.

I will tell you what I was: I was everything that was not the whiteness. I was my opposition, my resistance. The snow looked wonderfully inviting, Verena. Just one more step, I would tell myself, then you can lie down and rest. It doesn't matter if you never get up again. That one step will count. You will have done your job. No one can say otherwise.

The act of walking seemed strangely complicated. The snow was up to our knees. It stretched ahead as far as I could see, a pristine white surface carved by the wind. Loose powder rose like smoke. To take that one step I would have to extricate my foot from the snow, push it forward and then plunge it back down. It was just too much to ask. Only the promise of rest could make me go through all that again. To lie down seemed so wonderfully simple, and the implications no longer so terribly ominous. But if I did lie down, I did not want a big fuss—to be lectured, to be laid on top of the sledge—a useless gesture, and one we could no longer afford. Everyone already understood that. No, I imagined them removing my harness. I imagined watching the sledge move on without me, imagined it disappearing into the whirling snow. I imagined the snow covering me over, slowly at first, then more quickly, gaining speed till I was white, white, white.

But lying down was not so simple either. In order to lie down I first had to take that one step. That was the bargain I had made with myself. So I lifted my leg and then threw my weight forward against the harness, a kind of drunkard's lurch, kicking through the snow. And having done all that, having taken that one step, the very last blessed step of my life, I would then make myself do it all over again. That was the trick I used. Just one more step, one more step, and then you can lie down and rest. It doesn't matter if you never get up again. I went the last hundred miles that way.

She felt him hesitate, pause, recede and then return, as if he had decided to tell something he had not originally intended to.

On the way back we left Boyle in the snow. He was in bad shape, we all knew he wouldn't make it, so the next time he fell down we just kept going. No one said anything, it was just understood that we wouldn't look back.

He knew the risks.

Oh, yes, if it had only been that clean. The thing is, he actually caught up with us that night, when we were making camp, came in crawling on his hands and knees. In the tent the three of us huddled together for warmth with the man we had left to freeze on the ice, and when I woke he was dead. The first to go.

Jackson was the next to go. He limped alongside the sledge, unable to pull. It was just Portus and me in the harness now. At night in the tent, Jackson took off his boots and rubbed his feet with ice, trying to get the circulation back. They were black up to the ankles, and the smell was terrible, rank and fishy. Portus and I huddled together at the other end of the tent. "What do you think?" I whispered. I could not take my eyes off Jackson. His every gesture, his every move was fascinating. It was something about knowing that he would soon be dead, like Boyle, and something more—that he had the power to take us with him just by trying to stay alive.

But why?

There wasn't enough food, Verena. We had rations for five days, but the supply depot was nine or ten away, and he was slowing us down. He knew it too—he had turned around and left Boyle lying in the snow, just like the rest of us. "I don't see how he's gotten this far," said Portus. "Sheer willpower."

"We can't carry him."

"He knows that. He knows what he has to do." Just a few feet away, pretending not to hear, Jackson bent over his feet, rubbing them over and over with the ice, as if he could bring them back to life. But when I woke the next morning, he was already up, pulling on his boots. "What are you doing?" I asked him. "It's not light yet." But of course I knew.

"Going out for a stroll," was all he said, then undid the tent flap and left.

Where did he go?

God knows. Nowhere. Everywhere. We didn't look for him because we couldn't afford to find him.

With Jackson gone the equation changed. Both Portus and I grasped the logic: now that it was only the two of us we had enough food for another nine days, and since the supply depot was only ten days away, assuming the weather held up, we actually had a chance. And we almost made it. Portus died overnight, just two days march from the depot. I left him there and continued on alone for another day. That night the weather failed. I waited another two days alone in that tent, unable to leave. The silence was the roar of the storm. For the first time I understood what it was to be alone with your own devouring self. I had murdered those men so I could reach this point, and now all I wanted was to grasp that clam-shaped door knocker, and knock, and be allowed to enter. I did not want to linger by myself. I took off my snowsuit and felt the cold reach into me. You remember that first day we met?

At the arcade.

And the funny little electromagnetic contraption?

For a nickel. We both put a finger in.

And couldn't pull apart, no matter how hard we tried.

I didn't want to.

That's how it felt to die.

Verena lay in bed for some time, and then got up and peeked through the curtains at the street outside. The light had shifted down to the gold of late afternoon. Where had the hours gone? It would be evening soon, and then time for the séance.

She would have to dress. She ran her hand over the black gown as if it were flesh, as if it could feel her touch, and then very quickly began to fold—the arms pinned behind, the skirt gathered up. She found some muslin and used it as wrapping, as if covering a body in a shroud, and then opened the heavy wooden trunk in the corner of her closet. The fragrance of cedar and wool was sad and rich. She placed the bundle inside and closed the lid.

She put the gray dress from the morning back on, thinking all the while of Theodore, of the complicated and painful way he had died—even as she was waiting at home, willing to love him. She thought of the mourners who would be coming that night to make the spirit circle, hungry for the electricity of grief. And then she thought of Mr. Auerbach, who would also be there, perched in his wheelchair like a bird ready for flight. She might ask him to stay for coffee, and they might even plan another drive.

hark
ABE SMITH

this evening the dew is shameful this bruised eyelid evening
the street lamps warm flicker nonplussed plus

two

I have merle h. on I allow a peppermint tea
to be written my longings circle in chants to boot
what are the chances one two three five hike
leaping in the spiked heel in the gravel oh o

I know a writing done for patience I know a writing doled
one salt crack at a time I know one for a woman
so she use legs soon soft frock sad me the heart to howl is wide there

when the next then alaska can bleep her telemarket accent

I keep

these fish tinted hours between dusk and
socked dark

      the bleep being *take a wolf to*

now hour one my great strength

now I'm clean

where I walk after shines

night

night don't ash on me now

Endlessly Rocking
Michael P. Branch

The day Eryn and I decided to have a kid we had, it's true, been drinking quite a lot of gin. Gin, the product of fermented juniper berries; juniper, the wild trees that surround our home in the high desert—*Juniperus osteosperma*, the seminal one. This is not to say that ours was an uninformed decision. On the contrary, the limes were especially fresh, and we were drinking that vacation gin in the blue bottle, so superior to the bargain hooch we hardly bother to drink back home. So it was under conditions of extreme lucidity that we resolved to procreate. As any transcendentalist or gin drinker will attest, these are the proper circumstances under which to make a sober determination about something as weighty as the eternal fate of one's sperm or eggs.

After a decade removed from my home in the South—instead floating around in the glaring sun and desiccating wind of the Great Basin desert—I had come, as we all eventually must, back to the sea, to the cradle that Walt Whitman rightly called endlessly rocking. The sea here was the late-winter Atlantic, gray-green and rolling along the delicate strand of North Carolina's Outer Banks, where I caught my first running bluefish at age nine. If you could see the Banks from the point of view of a cloud, they would look like an attenuated brushstroke of bone-white, pencil-thin sweeps modulating with graceful doglegs and bottleneck passes—a calligraphy of sand levitating off the big island of North America, and all of it changing with every storm. My main objective in coming here was to sit on the chilly beach and stare at the world. Maybe study the tip of a surf rod stuck in a sand spike by the cooler. Maybe unwrap a C harp from a green bandana and bend a few blues lines around the booming G-ish bass of surf on sand. Maybe decide, once and for all, who would take the National League pennant in the upcoming season. Maybe resolve to have a child. It was a modest agenda, but I have always believed that with gin enough and time all problems are solvable. Or soluble: capable of being diluted with equal parts distilled juniper berries and seawater.

Michael P. Branch

Hiking on an exposed expanse of bare beach in March, squinting into the wind, pelted by flying sand, buried beneath the sound of roaring waves—this is surprisingly comforting to a desert dweller. If you can excuse there being water present, the rest is keenly familiar: leaning into the gust-driven gyre that lifts surging blasts of sand, you tilt toward a deep, gray horizon of dusty green swells that rise like shiny billows of mountain mahogany and creosote bush and bitterbrush—breakers undulating like shimmering waves of *Artemisa tridentata*, big sage, each three-lobed, succulent leaf reminiscent of Neptune's trident. Even the distant battleship clouds rise in broken, serrated ridgelines like desert mountains, low ranges lipping an almost overflowing world-round cup that holds both bluefish and pronghorn.

It is best to visit visited places when they are unvisited, not only to avoid the throng of fellow apes who shatter the mystic solitude necessary for problem solving—and questions of pennant races and child bearing promise to be close calls this year—but precisely because we most enjoy people's presence in registering their absence. I'm no misanthrope, but the best kind of solitude is created when other people leave. Even in praising the beauty of a "deserted" beach we reveal the awareness that it was once inhabited—betray the recognition that its charm is created not by its beauty alone, but also by the people who might be there but aren't, who once were there but have now deserted, blown away, moved on to crowd somebody else's beach where the folks there won't be able to solve a damned thing.

Melville observed that all paths lead to water—that an irresistible force constantly and silently pulls us, benighted terrestrialites, back to our watery home. Even in the desert it is true that all paths end either at a glistening spring or a pile of powdery bones. Like everything else in life, it's a simple matter of choosing the correct fork in the canyon's sandy, wash-bottom game trail. But there is something ineffably compelling about this limitless mass of life-filled water, roiling around the globe, pulled by moon and pushed by wind. It is a truism that we carry the ocean in our veins and tears, but that seems a thinly clinical way to measure the affiliation. My body is a gin-powered carbon-based flesh-satchel that is essentially saltwater—so far so good. But think of the *wildness* of the sea, with its innumerable underwater canyons and mountain peaks, its turreted and gabled reefs, its fissures and crypts, vents and vaults. Think of a myriad of minute life forms spiraling around towering spires of kelp, of the high-pressure, frigid, eternal darkness above which bright, fish-filled rivers of animated current run. Think of the battle between sperm whale and giant squid that is raging in the depths somewhere at this moment, the giant cephalopod frenetically twining its eighty-foot tentacles around the snapping jaws of a hundred-foot cetacean that is glaring, coldly, out of its tiny, bad-ass eye.

But think, too, of ourselves. Of how we crawled, frame by frame, time-lapse, out of the pond, rose to our feet, grabbed an ash or maple bat just as our flippers became digitized hands, and smacked a soaring dinger into the right-field bleachers—or invented the quadrant, or wrote *Hamlet*, or split the atom, or created the TV sitcom, or whatever you think of as the high point of hominid evolution. And just when a giant squid seems the ultimate nasty neighbor, try living on the land for a while, always worried about finding shade and fresh water and paying rent and taxes, flinching constantly at all the looming things that can spear you through the back of the neck while you're just trying to grub a few roots. Maybe the whale and its air-breathing marine cousins got it right when they crawled back into the drink: any sensible terrestrial mammal will tell you that leaving the pond wasn't exactly a cakewalk.

As I slice another lime with my bait knife, I think to myself that what would be wildest—and what would connect us with the wildness of our watery home even more powerfully than knowing that we cry salt tears—would be to crawl back in. Not in an underwater robot, like Jacques Cousteau, or with oxygen tanks on our backs, like Sean Connery's Bond, James Bond (somehow cool even in those standard-issue British agent diaper-white swim trunks), but silently and unassisted, simply breathing water as we once did, returning calmly to the quiet of our coral caves, leaving the windy beach without regret. Deserting.

Since this doesn't seem possible—although the manatees and dolphins have managed it rather gracefully—I've been contemplating the terrestrial mammal's best alternative: my wife's suggestion that perhaps we should resolve to give birth to a tiny human. This proposition seems at once perfectly natural and extremely reckless. For us non-marine mammals, being a fluid-breathing fetus at sea in the amniotic ocean of our mother's uterus is as close as we'll ever get to turning our backs on this troubled land and slithering back into the silent sea. Still, I can't help but think of the more mundane implications: how long does it take before a thing like that can run a weed whacker, cut stove wood, or limes even? My father always said that the perfect age for a kid is when they're old enough to run the lawnmower but not old enough to drive the car. Fair enough, but think of the magnitude of the investment, given the extremely narrow, pre-automotive mowing phase of child development. And these infants—what, exactly, do they *do* all day? And doesn't much of what they do smell? I've heard poet Galway Kinnell's scatophilic assertion that those who don't poop don't live, while those who do do do do do. But still.

As I look out over Walt's endlessly rocking cradle and consider this question further, I no longer picture the epic battle of cetacean and cephalopod, or the lovely, swaying towers of kelp, but instead imagine a pudgy little human baby, rosy-cheeked, bulging-eyed and wide-smiled, wearing bunchy diapers attached with those big pins (for some reason), and doing the breaststroke underwater as a curtain of bubbles periodically covers its fat face like a belch. An amphibious cherub, more monstrous than cute and not at all as advertised. As the thing swims slowly toward me with its trusting grin, I think how unlikely it is to survive very long down there, with all the hungry fish-folk, so red in tooth and fin—and it so corpulent and awkward and slow-moving, and probably not too chewy. Do I really want to take responsibility for this defenseless monster—neither fish nor ape—that can't hide in a coral nook, or outswim a shark, or even cut a lime? I'll mow my own god-damn lawn.

As the tiny beast paddles yet closer, a huge mushroom of brown bubbles suddenly bursts from beneath its diaper, blowing the diaper to shreds in underwater slo-mo. I suspect that sharks can smell this. I wince and turn away in disgust. Lifting the fruit jar from the sand I take a healthy belt of G&T, then slowly open my eyes and look out across the sea again. Somewhere beneath its rocking green cradle is a hypothetical baby—an amphibious infant that, like me, has saltwater in its veins and tears. I look beneath the surf again: against a trailing curtain of brown butt-chum it is still swimming at me placidly, still approaching land, ready to crawl out and stand up and swing a bat. And it is still grinning.

The woman who calls me her husband is from California, which isn't her fault. She's one of the Crackers of the West, that good Okie stock whose kin came across the Great Basin and Sierra like Ma and Pa Joad, piloting a ramshackle jalopy and looking for the endless orchards of what everybody from Moses to Chuck Berry called the Promised Land. But Eryn isn't blonde and she doesn't surf. As it turns out, California is loaded with brunettes and Christians, several of whom are not Republicans, and many of whom are non-surfers. Who knew? I'm a Virginian, and like many Southerners, what I know about California I learned from TV. Of course it is true that from my shack in the Blue Ridge I could receive only one TV station (by squeezing fistfuls of aluminum foil on the rabbit ears), and the picture came in so fuzzy that only in certain weather could I extract human shapes from the shimmering field of flying particles. The fact that Eryn didn't have the good sense to be a Southerner is, of course, more than a little embarrassing to me. But the fact that she's a Californian—this is something to be avoided in polite conversation. When my buddies back home in Virginia found out I was to be hitched, their first response was to ask me to give the woman their condolences (they didn't use the word "condolences"). But when they heard me mutter under my breath "California" in answer to the first question Southerners always ask about anybody—"Where did you say she was from?"—there was invariably dead silence on the line. Silence, followed by blasts of self-ironizing neo-hick lines, like "Boy, now you gonna hafta take up that surfin'!" I had a stock reply to this grilling, though I always worried that I delivered it with a defensiveness that was too obvious: "Her kin picked peaches, you dumb ass. You ever seen *Grapes of Wrath*?" Here was something my Virginia friends could understand; even if they weren't sure where Hollywood ended and California began, they knew what it was to pick peaches all day in the sun. Besides, they reasoned, it wasn't like I'd gone and married a Yankee, or worse, a Yankees fan. Damned carpetbaggers.

Eryn is the kind of woman who makes you want to do a fool thing like get married, even if you've had a good, long run of knowing better than to enter what I once disparagingly referred to as "the condition." Make no mistake, marriage is one of the few institutions I respect. Emerson was right that most institutions are dead forms: ossified, lumbering, impersonal, ineffective, inertial, disingenuous, self-promoting, tautological, hermetic, superficial, and fucked up (Emerson didn't actually say "fucked up," but that's what he was thinking). At a bus stop in Richmond I once saw an old drunk who was preaching, most righteously, into the noise of traffic: "Brother, beware the institution, for there's two things, *two things* that it never can do, *never can do*, and that is anything, *anything*, for the first or the last time . . . *first or last*, brother, first or last, *beware!*" There are prophets everywhere. I don't think the crazy wise man intended his divinely inspired admonition to apply to the institution of marriage, which is, as even lascivious old Ben Franklin recognized, a fine condition into which even freedom loving men should enter. But it somehow never seemed a good idea for *me* to enter it. Marriage wasn't like baseball—a game meant to be both played and watched—but rather like horse racing, something you only watched, and wagered on, and drank at, but didn't actually participate in. Besides, as my friend JJ used to argue, weddings are the ideal venue for an entrepreneurial bachelor: you tank free booze while watching another man lose his freedom and you usually end up with a companionable female who always has to go home to somewhere else the next morning. Why would a guy want to mess up something like that by having his own wedding?

Even with the weight of the evidence regarding "the condition" on the other side of the question, I married Eryn—or, more accurately, she was generous enough to marry me. It is also true that the night of our wedding, when we all stayed at the rundown mountain lodge where the hitchfest took place, my unmarried buddies from below the Mason-Dixon Line raked our deep stock of liquor absolutely clean before engaging in unconscionably loud sex with every Okie they could get out of a dress—which at least increased their appreciation for Leftcoast produce other than peaches. When squaring up with the lodge I was asked to pay $125 extra for a broken bed, which I did without asking questions.

Eryn is smart, patient, and wonderfully generous. She's also witty, stubborn, and optimistic. And though she is Californian, her non-blondeism and non-surfishness, combined with her peach-picking lineage in the Central Valley—the "Appalachia of the Golden State"—are substantially redeeming. She's a good friend, and she's resourceful and interesting, which is saying something. It would have been good if I had thought of some of this stuff to put in my crappy, bootlegged, eleventh-hour wedding vows—if you're hungover and you end-run the Bible you're left with shit for vows, as it turns out. We've been married two years and two months—precisely the same amount of time ornery Thoreau lived on the banks of Walden Pond—and I've about decided this is the best way a man can live. I love being married to Eryn. She turned out to be the peach at the top of the tree, the one worth waiting for, even if her weedy roots didn't grow in southern soil.

But just as I'm feeling at peace with my new and improved life, the specter of the swimming diaper-blasting insanely grinning non-lime-slicing not-yet-lawnmowing amphibious proto-dinger-smacking belching cherub has come upon me from right field—a place things should go to, not come from. Somehow this strikes me as unfair. I mean, I've just taken a deep breath and said yes, by golly, I'm pretty darned pleased about this whole marriage condition, when this fat-faced hypothetical baby comes along, with all its expulsing bodily fluids, to sour my gin and trouble the wide oceans and attract poop-sniffing sharks. It was like sliding safely across home plate and *then* being tagged out, and by the umpire. But safety, so hard to come by in this world, is especially elusive when freakish babies are paddling around the juniper juice-bath in your noggin.

It happened this way. Eryn and I had just come back from a nearly ideal lovers' evening walk along the chilly, deserted strand of beach with my dog, a thick-headed mystery mutt she kindly called "good-natured." I should explain that I had vexed my family by foolishly naming the dog "Cat," which I thought sounded cool (as in "cool cat, dude"), but which I bestowed primarily, and smugly, to illustrate the power of behavior modification and operant conditioning. "This dog doesn't *think* about the fact that it's a dog," I philosophized over a beer one summer afternoon after returning from the pound with the new addition to the family. "Hell, I could call him 'Cat,' and he'd still come when I called him, so long as he was trained, like Pavlov's dog, with a clearly structured series of rewards and punishments." Well, by the time the words tumbled out of my mouth I was already in trouble. First of all, it should have occurred to me that this sort of conditioning had failed when my folks tried it on me. In characteristic form, that morning at the campsite Cat had licked the coagulated sausage grease out of the bottom of the frying pan while I was taking a leak on the other side of the dune, and when we later took him down to the ocean he immediately rushed into the surf, attacked the first wave he could reach as it broke on shore, shotgunning a bucketful of ocean as a chaser for his slimy breakfast, after which he dragged along all morning, puking up sand, saltwater, and sausage grease as he went. Cat may have been "good-natured," but he was sufficiently dim-witted to remind me constantly of Mark

Twain's incisive remark that "if I was co-owner of that dog, I'd shoot my half." So despite what I claimed to know about the power of behavior modification, the Pavlov horseshit backfired, leaving me stuck with a dog named Cat who was a moron but who was just smart enough to know that he had been badly named by a dumb-ass smart-ass, which he didn't like one bit.

So we had just come back from this great evening walk along the beach, and we were sitting in the tent as a light sea breeze rippled the sloping nylon walls, and the glow of the rising moon poured through the mesh windows, making it bright enough for me to find my limes. We were half-tucked into our sleeping bags as evening damp began to fall, and we were on the sandy shoulder of the infinite sea, and we were laughing, and we were simultaneously drinking and playing gin. Cat, now snoring loudly in the corner of the tent—another bad habit of his that I forgot to mention—had even stopped yacking. I was fully inhabiting the role of the proverbial happily married man. In short, the situation was as close to ideal as it is likely to get on this side of the veil of tears.

"Did you ever think about having a baby?" Eryn asked, absolutely unprovoked. I could hear her voice winging in from right field, as I stood, incredulous, once again tagged out after safely crossing the plate. At that exact moment I was slicing a lime, and I damn near cut my finger off, though it did flash through my mind that if nine and a half fingers was good enough for Jerry Garcia it ought to be good enough for me.

"Huh?" I replied, cribbing my eloquent rejoinder from chapter one of *The Husband's Handbook*. Before she could rephrase the question I rebounded, wittily, "I'd like to, but I don't think it's anatomically possible. Perhaps you've mistaken me for a seahorse?"

"Michael, be serious," she said. My long first name plus a command, encapsulated incisively in a three-word sentence. This was inauspicious. Happily married man meets buzz-crushingly serious topic of adult conversation.

"Hey, feel free to call me 'Mike.' Besides, what do you want with one of those?" I asked, desperately invoking levity where it had so little chance of success. "I hear they're expensive and noisy and they smell bad. Really, things are so perfect right now."

"But maybe they would be *more* perfect if we were a real family,"

Eryn said with disturbing sincerity.

I objected, grasping at semantic straws. "You can't have 'more perfect'—'perfect' is as good as it gets. Besides, we *are* a real family. What are you talking about? Look at us: *happy family*!" At this moment I spontaneously spread both arms wide apart, gesticulating grandly to suggest the impressive expansiveness of said happy family, when the gin-soaked gyroscope in my inner ear caused me to lose my balance and, as I fell over, snag my hand on the taut laundry cord above me, spilling my icy drink in my crotch while catapulting a pair of moderately used tighty-whities, formerly on the line, onto the extended snout of the sleeping Cat, who first snuffled and then farted loudly.

I looked up at my sweet wife, who looked back in silence at my undoubtedly plaintive expression, and my soaked crotch, and my strewn underwear, and my farting dog, and then dropped her pretty forehead into her open palm to hide a smile. She had to be fantasizing about what her life was like before she married me.

"Let me think on it some," I said.

"Okay," she replied, looking up with a labored straight face. "Now cut the lime—the round green one, mind you, not the long, brown one with the fingernail on it. It's your deal." In that moment I remember thinking, very clearly: I really love this woman. I freshened our drinks, snuggled down into my bag, removed the tee-dubs from Cat's snout and placed them, officiously, upside-down on my head, waistband-as-headband style, and began to deal a hand of gin, and to sing an old Sleepy John Estes song: "When that wind, that chilly breeze, come blowin' through your BVDs, you gotta move, you gotta move chile, you gotta move." And, inspired by my flapping lid, I'm singing the blues with what I take to be the accent of a French chef.

I was pretty sure that adults didn't sit in tents, half-drunk, with gin-soaked balls, wearing underwear on their heads, losing repeatedly at gin, and singing the blues in Franco-phony. Adults, I was pretty sure, made mature decisions about things like whether or not to have children. Long after Eryn went to sleep I was still singing mournful old Sleepy John: "There's change in the ocean, a change in the sea, I declare now, Mama, there'll be a change in me, well everybody, they ought to change sometime, because sooner or later, you got to go down in that lonesome ground." Bless you, Sleepy John.

But of course I wasn't sleepy. As I lay in my bag listening to the breakers walk up the beach under the high pull of the big moon, I thought about change, and love, and water. These are expansive topics, I know, but I tend to sleep about four hours less each night than Eryn, which gives me plenty of extra time for these contemplations—1,460 hours extra per year, to be exact, the equivalent of sixty days, in effect an extra two months per annum of dangerously abstract and self-absorbed metaphysical musings. In fact, my unique habit of combining strong java, Mountain Dew, hard liquor, and excessive contemplation makes me an excellent candidate for spontaneous human combustion. Anyway, I once pointed out to Eryn that, thanks to my superhuman frenetic insomnia, I'd get in *years* more of sentient contemplations than she would before they threw the dirt on the box. Her reply, without hesitation: "What if you're only given a certain number of waking hours in your mortality allowance? You're squandering time thinking in circles about the shape of the universe, while I'm having wonderful dreams about being a kid again." As usual, she had a point. But I couldn't sleep anyway, so I lay there singing Sleepy John, listening to the ocean and to that damned snoring dog and thinking about change, and love, and water.

Water. We're made of it, it surrounds us, and we buy the farm if we go more than a few days without taking some of it in or even without squirting some of it out. Mark Twain said that "whiskey is for drinking and water is for fighting over," and W. C. Fields, pontificating wryly about water while drinking rye, claimed he "never touched the stuff" because, as he put it so memorably, "fish fuck in it." But there's a good reason why a guy with a name like McKinley Morganfield would call himself Muddy Waters. You wouldn't see a guy named Muddy Waters changing his name to McKinley Morganfield because he'd end up being an accountant rather than wailing the blues. Face it, we wouldn't get far—physically or imaginatively—without water. Newborns must revisit the hydrant of their mother's breast a dozen times a day, and old men must make pilgrimages to the places they swam and fished and paddled in their youth before they can die well. Well . . . another place from which life-giving water flows.

I think of old friends who were pulled to water. Not just Herman in the South Pacific and Henry at the pond and Walt crossing Brooklyn Ferry, but also Mister Jefferson admiring the dramatic confluence of the Potomac and Shenandoah, Lewis and Clark portaging around the sublime falls of the Missouri, Twain dodging snags in deep fog on the moonlit Mississippi. One-armed John Wesley Powell lashed in his straight-backed chair to the deck of a wooden boat shooting the gorges of the unknown Colorado. Crazy Hemingway cruising the Caribbean in a fishing boat he had outfitted to attack German U-boats. Brother John Muir trying in vain to explain the sacredness of Hetch-Hetchy water, or Cactus Ed Abbey floating the unspeakable beauty of Glen Canyon before it was buried beneath sunburned water skiers. Norman McLean reaching with the tip of a fly rod to touch the heart of his lost brother on the Big Blackfoot. And I think, especially, of young Nathaniel Hawthorne, sitting in the upper window of the Old Manse in Concord, looking up from his manuscript and out to the sweeping bend of the Concord River as it glides through swollen spring meadows and under the wooden arch of the Old North Bridge. He had just become a father, and he was ecstatic with joy and creative energy.

"Rise and whine, Bubba," said my wife, through the sound of the ocean beyond her. I wriggled out of my sleeping bag, crawled out of the tent, and stood up, bleary but proud in my American flag boxer shorts, out of which fell a desiccated slice of lime. "Eeeew," Eryn said, exaggerating for effect as she handed me a cup of cowboy coffee. Cat sniffed the leathery lime, licked it up off the sand, then spat it out again, shaking his head a little. I pulled on some clothes and looked out at the ocean. The breeze was up and the surf was up and now I was up too. Three gulls were turning above us on the spokes of an invisible wheel, and a few light clouds on the horizon said good weather. It was chilly, but not nearly as cold as I had expected it to be.

After breakfast Eryn instructed me to go fishing, which is another of her many fine qualities. "Take your gear and your limes and whatever nastiness it is you use for bait, and go stare at the world. That's why you came, right? I'm going to read, and discuss current events with Cat, the boy genius. Come back whenever." So off I went, shuffling along the shore with my sandspike and rod in one hand, my little cooler in the other, and my libational daypack on my back. Because I was raised as a fisherman and also as a slave to a Puritanical work ethic, I must fish in order to think—or to think about something other than how lazy I'm being by just thinking instead of doing something productive, like fishing. So I was following a comfortable routine, except that now I had the burdensome assignment of thinking about progeny, which seemed an intimidating subject of contemplation, especially for vacation. Setting up by the deserted seashore, I sat in the sand and stared at the world, as planned, and I fished and thought, as usual. And although I had pleasant, solitary meditations on the subjects of water and baseball and evolution, I ultimately began to envision the vulnerable, belching, defecating, grinning underwater ape-baby I've already mentioned. Unable to shake this horrid vision I decided to forgo the pleasures of angling—old Izaak Walton would have been scandalized—and instead trudged back to camp by afternoon. I had decided that procreation is a subject more fit for lively discussion than solipsistic contemplation, and so I reckoned that, given her central role in the would-be plan, it would be best if Eryn had an opportunity to weigh in on the subject.

Despite my disturbing vision and unproductive musings, I had struck upon one brilliant idea: if I could imagine a *name* for the child that we might, perhaps, possibly someday have at some unspecified time in the future, I could humanize, *personalize* the thing, thus making it easier to imagine it without having weird visions. "Baby," "infant," "toddler": words that cause mild discomfort and definitely sound like they would trigger the need for substantial responsibility. But somehow it didn't sound so bad to hang around and listen to a ball game on the radio with "Joe" or "Jane." No big deal. Then they mow the lawn a couple times and go off to college, right? So I entered camp with what I took to be a superb conversation starter: baby names.

"Honey," I asked, setting my rod and spike aside by the tent, "if we did have a kid, what would you want to name it?" She stared at me blankly.

"That's what you came up with after contemplating the great sea?"

"No, really. You know how when you have a name for something or somebody that's nameless, you know, anonymous, like a disease that you have, or somebody like a criminal, it really humanizes the whole thing?" I urged.

"A *disease* or a *criminal*?"

"Okay, bad examples. But just for fun, come on, let's talk about what names you like. Let's sit down in the sand and work on this a little. I'll mix the G&Ts, you start tossing out some names. Let's say it's a girl. Whatcha got?" She paused and looked at me a little suspiciously, but she couldn't resist, which was when I first realized she had already been thinking about the dangerous subject of kid names. So we sat, facing each other, a light breeze easing down the dune and the rocking ocean stretching out beyond us to the sky.

"Well, I had a wonderful great aunt on my mother's side who I really loved, Aunt Mabel," she said, with inexplicable seriousness.

"*Mabel*," I choked, "thou shittest me, yes?"

"Well, okay, how about Phyllis—it means 'leafy bow' in Greek. I think that's pretty."

"Even if that name didn't immediately bring to mind Phyllis Diller, don't you think somebody would call her 'Sy-phyllis'? No, we don't want Phyllis Diller or syphilis around—especially not Phyllis Diller *and* syphilis. Lordy."

"Well, what about something fun, like Jasmine?" she suggested in frustration.

"Perfect! That is, if you want your daughter to be a hooker. Hey, we could just name her Jasmine Syphilis; of course, we'd never get affordable health insurance on somebody with a name like that."

Eryn was enjoying this exchange, though she also enjoyed pretending—with dramatic obviousness—that she wasn't. "Okay, Mister Veto, what names do *you* like?"

This was a predictable turn in the discussion but, as usual, I was unprepared for it anyway. I tried to buy some time: "Did I ever tell you about the time I went to Sleepy Hollow Cemetery in Concord to visit the graves of Emerson and Thoreau? No? Alright, well I made a pilgrimage to the holy burying place, called Author's Ridge, a beautiful, breezy knoll, covered with white pines and, well, dead writers. It was a beautiful day, midsummer, and I had just come from skinny-dipping in Walden Pond. Emerson's headstone is this big-ass rock—just a giant, unhewn granite boulder. Thoreau, on the other hand, is napping under this dinky little stone that just says 'Henry.' Tasteful, you know. Modest, restrained—definitely not too showy. Still, you'd think they could have taken up a collection or something. Even Hawthorne and Alcott had better stones than Henry."

"So you want to name our daughter Henrietta?"

"*As I was saying*, once I checked out the big boys up on the ridge, I decided to wander around the graveyard looking for the oddest name I could find. Believe me, there were some pretty funkified old-fashioned names there. But when I found what I was looking for, I knew I couldn't possibly do better, and to this day I've never forgotten her name." I paused. "Are you ready for this?" Again, dramatic pause. "Fucius Barzilla Holdenballs."

She rolled her eyes. "First, I don't believe you. Second, that's got to be a boy's name. And third, it wouldn't be pronounced 'Fewshus'—it would be 'Fewkaius.'"

"First, I swear on the grave of Fucius Barzilla Holdenballs," I said, moving my drink to my left hand so I could raise my right in a solemn pledge, "that I have spoken the gospel truth. Second, I don't know how you could think that Barzilla is a guy's name. And, third, only an Okie with strong Old Testament leanings could get 'Fewkaius' out of 'Fewshus.'"

"Well, which of these delightful names are you proposing for your poor daughter? Not Holdenballs, certainly?"

"Witty," I said with fake condescension. "I had to marry the witty one." She smiled, a little proudly. I was out of time. "How about Melissa," I offered spontaneously. I had been singing Allman Brothers tunes while fishing, and it was all I could think of besides Fucius Barzilla Holdenballs, which had clearly played out by now.

"No good. People will call her Mel, and then everybody will think she's a boy—and a truck driver, or a short-order cook." I hesitated, thinking about the fact that two of my best friends were engaged in these noble occupations. But I had thought of a good follow-up name, until Eryn continued: "Besides, Melissa is like Jessica, it just sounds kind of trashy."

She had an uncanny way of anticipating and blocking my next move, though I suppose I shouldn't have stuck inflexibly with Allman Brothers song titles. But I loved those smooth, sonorous, sibilant, southern names. Maybe because they were trashy, I don't know. "Well, how about 'Althea,'" I blurted.

"Althea! That's what you named your guitar!"

"Well, yeah, but it's a great name." She stared me down with that great fake serious look of hers. "I could rename my ax. No, never mind." I really didn't want to rename my guitar. That would be like renaming your dog—which I obviously would have done long ago if I could have. I'd just have to figure out the girl's name without borrowing from any of my instruments, pets, or nicknames for body parts.

The longer this went on the more I realized that if I were to become the father of a daughter, I would be compelled, about sixteen years from now, to kick the ass of somebody who would probably look and act exactly like me. I quickly retrieved and refiled for future use the first line my father-in-law had used in welcoming me into his home: "Howdy, son, let me show you my gun collection." But beneath the laughter of the name game I felt a real fear, some impossible-to-describe sense that I wasn't ready, or, more accurately, that I somehow just wouldn't know what to do—that I'd be a bumbling father to a baby girl, a flawed, obsessive father to a girl kid, an alien species to a teen-aged woman. Now I could feel the limey G&T, which I had ingested with a fair amount of sand, begin to roil in my gut. Maybe the escape hatch was to imagine being a father to a son instead? I knew this wasn't something you could count on, but I figured the odds weren't any worse than the ones people wager on at the roulette table—though I also realized that the simple choice of red or black didn't involve diapers or saving for college, and would, at least, come with free drinks. Still, it seemed worth a try.

"This ain't workin'," I said. "How about boys' names? Whatcha got?"

"Philip!" she said without hesitation.

I just shook my head.

"An excellent choice if you want to avoid having grandchildren. But at least it would be handy to have an interior decorator in the family. I just hope the leotard isn't too expensive."

"You're appalling," she said. "Well, what about Jeremiah? You've always liked strong names," she said.

"Strong, yes; apocalyptic, no. I'd feel like it was the last supper every time I called the kid for dinner: 'Oh, Jeremiah, boy, on the way home from school, could you ask the Lord to have mercy on Daddy's soul? Now put down your flaming cross and go mow the lawn, then get washed up for your fishes and loaves.' On the other hand"—and now I leaned over toward her, half turned for dramatic effect, and sang loudly—"Jeremiah was a bullfrog! A lot of people wouldn't want to have a son who is a bullfrog," I said, "but I'm very accepting. To *Rana catesbiana*. Long may he jump!" We raised our plastic glasses in a silent toast.

"So, McBluffer, you don't have a single decent name, do you?" she asked, starting the next round.

"Nope. I've got three: Diogenes Asclepiades Themistocles."

"That's Greek to me, unless it's one of those joke names, like the novel *Over the Cliff* being by Hugo First."

"Nope. Real name. Means 'fat man with healthy testicles.' Believe me, you could do worse—with those fine testes you'd have good prospects for grandchildren. Philip can't hold a candle to this guy. How about Hugo?"

"I had to marry the witty one," she said, smiling. "Let's eat. Maybe we're too famished to think clearly."

"Impossible! We're drinking the juice of junipers and limes here—vegetables and fruits, very nutritious. Come on, one last shot at naming the poor boy. Let's use the trusty blues naming formula—works especially well for boys." She knew it was a trap, but she didn't care. We were by the great ocean, our ancestral home, and we were with our dog, such as he was, and we were drinking G&Ts with fresh lime and sitting in the sand. And, in our own laughing, indirect way, we were discussing the idea of starting a family.

"Whatcha got?" she asked, knowing how much I would enjoy this. It was like hitting a homer off a tee, but it still felt great.

"Here's the formula: disability plus fruit or vegetable plus last name of U.S. President. Works every time—you know, as in haunted Texas bluesman Blind Lemon Jefferson." This was an example Eryn could appreciate, since my own blues nickname, given to me by buddies who wanted to encourage my blues harp playing while also forcing me to maintain absolute humility, was a riff on this one: "Blind Lemon Pledge."

"Give it a try," I said, with sincere encouragement in my voice.

"Deaf . . . Watermelon . . . Washington." She grinned.

"Perfect! Deef Melon, get in this house and eat your macaroni and cheese! Deef Melon, you damned rounder, you be in by ten!" We toasted again, our plastic cups coming together silently as we cheered ourselves. Cat, disturbed by our laughter, opened one eye briefly before he resumed snoring.

"Hey, how about Bald Pineapple Wilson?" she offered. "Bald Pineapple, you get out there and mow the lawn this minute! Bald Pineapple, put a little elbow grease into those dirty dishes!"

I continued: "Bald Pineapple, if I catch you hangin' around the crossroads 7-eleven I'll slice your noggin and put toothpicks in the pieces! Why, now, Bald Pineapple, I can't *believe* you got a D in math . . . way to go!" I could hardly speak for laughing. I truly think if we had given birth to a child that moment I would have insisted on "Bald Pineapple." It somehow seemed perfect. Then again, everything seemed perfect. And though I recalled briefly that this sort of enthusiasm had caused my dog to be named Cat, and my previous dog to be named L. Ron Hubbard, I really did have my heart suddenly set on Bald Pineapple.

"Bowlegged Broccoli Adams!" Eryn said.

"Specify Adams," I insisted, sounding serious.

"John, of course. The other one is Crippled Quince Adams," she replied instantly.

"I remember now, he ended up in a jam."

"Pigeon-toed Asparagus Taft," she continued.

"Is that the one they used to call Stinky Pee?" I asked.

"The very same. And they said he'd never amount to anything. He was in office just after Rheumatoid Brussels Sprout Roosevelt."

"Teddy, then?" I said, again calling for clarification.

"Of course. FDR was much later—you know, Flatulent Dewberry Roosevelt." We both looked at Cat and laughed.

"Of course. He filled the power vacuum created by Hoover," I said. She smiled.

"Right. Psychotic Carrot Hoover. He was quite unstable, but he had great vision in a dark time, may he rest in peace," she said, grieving his loss momentarily until she broke out laughing again. Now neither of us could stop laughing at the fact that the other was laughing so hard at something so ridiculous. Of course we knew that none of this was actually funny, but we didn't care, which made us laugh even more. I suppose this is the irrational nature of joy.

"Wife," I heard myself say unexpectedly, "do you think I'd be a good father?"

"Yes, Bubba, I do." She smiled. I paused, laughed quietly, and then lowered my head and nodded it left to right—but I meant yes, the way you shake your head and raise your eyebrows and laugh before you start skiing down or climbing up the biggest, most beautiful mountain you've ever seen in your life.

I sat quietly now, washed over by a feeling of certainty. Eryn's face was glowing as it must have when she was a curly-headed little baby girl, and the woman who calls me her husband never looked so beautiful before. I could see her as a child, as a mother, and as an old woman. I could hear the swaying ocean and feel the evening breeze and see the bone moon lifting slowly out of the dunes. I was immersed in the moment and yet also somehow already looking back at it with deep satisfaction, like I was already seeing this place and time from an old wicker rocker, rocking with my old wife, endlessly rocking, ninety years old on some crooked porch with my old wife—maybe toothless and incontinent, but somehow happy anyway, and happier still to have the great gift of one clear memory of the moment I was now living. It was like sitting backwards in the bed of a speeding pickup: the first moment you see what's around you it is already racing toward the receding horizon. But there is no separating thrill from disappearance, gift from risk, growth from loss. Life speeds away, or we speed away from it, and only in moments like these can we wrinkle up our lives to make the good parts touch—warp the linear narrative of days to see ourselves being told by a larger story that isn't finished yet.

When our daughter was born we called her Hannah Virginia. Hannah, an ancient name meaning "grace," and a name that makes sense forward and backward, as she races into the unknown future and then returns in her own growing memories of the past. Virginia, the name of the homeland I carry inside me everywhere I go, as I hope she too will have a homeland inside her always. Hannah is two years and two months old now, and she knows the call of meadowlark and mountain bluebird and raven, the flower of lupine and desert peach and buckwheat, the shine of bluish Vega, the reddish glow of Arcturus, the spiral light of Venus. She can distinguish the rounded scat of the jackrabbit from the woodrat's oval pellets and the coffee beans left by pronghorn. She loves Cat, and she knows that he's a dog. What is most important to her, she explained to me today, is that she wants to grow as tall as the basin wild rye. She loves the beach and the sound of its cradle-rocking waves, and her laughter every day is the blossom of the seeds of love once sown in sand.

Ghost Lights
Sarah Blackman

At first she traces patterns on his chest—a cross, five-pointed stars, boxes, boxes, boxes. Later, after the first and the second, the fifth time they've slept together she stops reaching higher than his nipple, rounding for a thicker waist. Outside, it is a waste of summer. Mockingbirds dip the phone lines, ride electricity. What a time for a train and a lightning bolt, an old tree, sick tires, the lawnmower coughing, slide of a body, the pattern in the sheets. Take a picture to see the ghost lights. They are all around this house and hovering. Caught up in the old tree, low in the grass. On the porch she smokes cigarettes and tells him how little she needs him in her life.

Eye. Arm. Leg. Heart.
REBECCA BARRY

It was his liver, hardened by five thousand gallons of eighty-proof gin, that finally killed Harlin Wilder.

The sharp pang of loneliness Harlin's first wife Janine felt when she heard this news surprised her. Her marriage to Harlin, which had lasted barely eight months, had ended more than a decade ago, and Janine had long since put that time behind her. Still, when Harlin's lawyer, Lanford Guthrie, drove out to her mother's house to tell her Harlin was gone, Janine sat down at her kitchen table and put her head in her hands.

Lanford, who was a polite man, took a flask of whiskey out of his coat pocket and handed it to her. "It's a sad thing," he said. "They don't make them like Harlin anymore."

Janine felt the liquid go down and remembered how much she'd loved whiskey. She'd given up hard liquor years ago when she became a nurse, but she missed her old habits. Now, the whiskey warming her blood, she looked at the barn across the street, sagging in the middle as if it understood her. Harlin had remained in her memory as one of those fantastic alcoholics who never died, one of those flukes of nature that just kept on drinking long after the joggers and vegans died of heart attacks. And here was Lanford Guthrie, a drinker himself whom Janine had known since high school, a man she thought might have given in years ago, sitting in her kitchen alive and well and telling her that Harlin was gone.

"I represented him in court just this year," Lanford said. He was thin and wiry, with a bony, dignified face and thick black hair that curled at the nape of his neck. "His wife was suing him because he took all her money to start up a petting zoo."

Janine laughed and handed back his flask. "What in the hell was he going to do with a petting zoo?" she said, although she had a pretty good idea. Harlin had always been a ridiculous optimist, certain he could make a lot of money if he could just find the right plan. "Let's go to Bermuda and make a million bucks chartering boats," he'd say. "Let's take that Airstream and make it into a traveling coffee shop." They weren't all bad ideas. Some of them were very good. Which was the worst part, since they all overlooked the fact that Harlin had terrible credit and very little follow-through.

"He got drunk one day and decided he was going to start this zoo out at his dad's old place," Lanford said. "He took Charlene's money out of her savings and spent it all on fencing supplies and animal feed."

"And beer for all the people he was going to hire," Janine said.

Lanford smiled. "Naturally," he said.

"Including you," Janine said. She meant to laugh when she said this, but then she began to cry. She had loved Harlin, and he had loved her, and even though that time had passed, she remembered his voice and his hands, and the way he couldn't get enough of her skin.

Lanford pulled a cocktail napkin out of his pocket, checked it for phone numbers, and, seeing none, handed it to Janine. He put his arm around her shoulders, and Janine smelled good whiskey and cigarettes, a smell she'd always liked on a man. She breathed it in from his jacket before she pulled away.

The funeral would be the next morning, Lanford said, downtown at the funeral home on Chestnut Street.

"You going?" Janine guessed the answer even before Lanford shook his head. The funeral would be full of his clients, she knew, and Lanford, who saw a little of himself in each one, wouldn't want to be closer to their lives than he already was.

"No," he said. "But Cyrus Wilder was out last night telling everyone it was going to be a big party."

Janine laughed and blew her nose. "I bet he was."

Lanford picked up his coat and draped it over his arm. "It's nice to see you, Janine," he said. "You look good."

"Thank you," she said. "It was nice of you to drive all the way out here to tell me about this."

"I was going by the jail anyway," Lanford said. He held his gaze steady, and Janine felt her face grow warm. "You should call me tomorrow, if you go to the funeral," he said.

It was a pass and Janine knew it, and for a minute she thought about reminding him that she was living with a cabinetmaker named Trey. But then she decided not to. It was rare these days that anyone, even Trey, looked at her the way Lanford did now, like she was a single, delicious, ripe piece of fruit.

"You're sweet to try, Lanford Guthrie," she said.

"Nothing sweet about it," he said, and left.

The funeral was at eleven, which was a bad choice, since most of the attendees had been out the night before and were still hungover. "It's not what Harlin would have wanted," said Rita Johnson, the first person Janine saw when she got out of her truck. Rita tended bar at Lucy's, where Harlin and Janine used to drink, and she embraced Janine warmly. "It's too goddamn early," she said. "If Harlin were alive, even he wouldn't have shown up."

Janine and Rita walked toward the funeral home, where it looked like there was an alcoholic's revival taking place. Two men staggered up to the porch looking like they might still be drunk. A woman who looked like she could lift a piano carried a cooler of beer. She had put her hair up in a knot and wore no eye makeup but lots of lipstick on wonderful red lips. There were other women, some in black, but some in lighter colors—pink, and light green, as if they refused to be dark on this occasion. Some men wore work clothes—clean Dickies pants and work boots. Others, hair slicked down and side-parted, carried containers of food.

There were a few faces besides Rita's that Janine recognized. Stewart Levine, who couldn't drive because of the metal plate in his head, rode in on his bicycle. He was wearing a brown corduroy suit that barely reached his ankles and was carrying a fistful of balloons that said "Congratulations!" on them. Cyrus Wilder, Harlin's older brother, walked up the stairs with his cousin Earl, who had thick glasses and wore a neck brace. Most of the faces, however, were only vaguely familiar, and Janine was reminded that it had been a long time since she'd been back to this part of town.

Janine and Rita went inside and took a seat between a nun and two men who looked like they'd been scooped off the pavement that morning. Harlin's sister Angie began the service by reading a piece from Corinthians. She had a plain, honest face and wore a shapeless dress with a collar that looked like a doily. The last time Janine had seen Angie was at a picnic for the volunteer fire department in 1989, when Angie had asked Janine if she thought twenty-five dollars was enough to charge a guy for letting him see her tits. "Ask for forty," Janine had said. "Settle for twenty-seven."

"What happened to her?" Janine whispered to Rita.

"She found God," Rita said.

Angie passed the microphone to her husband, who read a brief poem he'd written about God's love and then opened the floor to anyone who wanted to share words about Harlin.

Harlin's cousin Earl stood up and began a short speech about how he and Harlin had been friends since they were kids, and how he used to hang out with all the Wilder boys, partying, driving, shooting things, and calling each other brother.

"Harlin gave me this shirt," Earl said. It was a purple tie-dyed T-shirt with a wolf on it that said, If all the animals in the world were to be killed, human beings would die from the loss of spirit. What happens to the animals will eventually happen to the humans. Chief Takoma.

"He told me how his grandfather taught him to look at trees, drive a tractor, and shoot a gun." Earl started crying. "He loved nature. So that's Harlin. If anyone sees me walking around with this shirt on, you can come up and say hello to Harlin." Earl sat down sobbing, and Angie passed him a tissue.

"Shooting a gun isn't exactly the same as loving nature," Rita said. She passed Janine a shot of whiskey and offered some to the nun, who smiled and took an eensy sip.

A black woman in a lavender suit and matching pillbox hat stood up.

"I run the shelter around the corner," she said. "And I wouldn't have been able to get in touch with the homeless people around here if it hadn't been for Harlin." There were a few "Amens" from the crowd. So he was homeless at the end, thought Janine.

"And I know right now he's in a much better place than that hospital," the woman went on. "And he's probably still wearing that ugly leather jacket."

People laughed and a basket was passed around with sheets of paper so those who were shy could write something down. Janine couldn't think of what to write right away, so she peeked at what other people had written. "Harlin, I love you. Keep on riding the magic carpet." "Remember. A good man is never forgotten."

Janine thought about how, two nights before, her sister had asked her if her boyfriend was the love of her life. "How would I know?" She had said. "I'm not dead yet." But she had thought of Harlin then, as she thought of that exchange now. "Oh, Harlin," she wrote. "The world won't be the same without you." Then she remembered the time he lost his whole paycheck in a dogfight. "PS:" she wrote. "You owe me 200 bucks."

After the funeral, Rita went home to help her girlfriend with their vegetable garden and Janine followed the rest of Harlin's mourners to the wake, which was held at the Elk's Lodge down the street. In the lodge basement, people sat at long, cafeteria-style tables, with cans of beer and plates of macaroni and cheese, baked beans, and scalloped potatoes that came in tinfoil pans. In the back was a cake with a picture on it of the waterfall by the power plant where Harlin, according to many of the guests and the police officers present, often went to drink alone. It was probably, Janine guessed, where Cyrus and Earl were now, getting stoned in Harlin's honor—especially since the police officers were present and not out on their beats.

Janine sat down next to two women and two men who were eating macaroni salad from paper plates and drinking beer. The men introduced themselves as Rusty and Jack. They were young and hard boned with farmers' caps and jackets that smelled like wood smoke. Then they introduced the women, Cadence and Roxanne.

The group must have liked the look of Janine because they cleared a space for her and tried to make her comfortable. Cadence, the elder of the two, got up to fix Janine a plate of food while Roxanne, whom Janine recognized as the woman she'd seen earlier with the red lipstick carrying beer, offered her a cheese cube and some crackers. Janine put her sweater on the back of her chair and asked them all how they knew Harlin.

Jack, the rougher looking of the two men, said he'd met Harlin working on a road crew out on Route 17. Rusty said his birth mother had lived next to Harlin when he was a baby, but that he'd gotten to know Harlin at the horse auctions a few years back. Janine imagined the boy was good with horses. He was handsome—thin but muscular, as if he lifted boxes of coal for a living, with deep red-brown skin as if he had some Indian blood in him. There was a vulnerability about his expression and unkempt hair that Janine imagined put people and animals at ease.

"I met him when I was tending bar at Lucy's," Cadence said. She had intelligent eyes and the gravelly voice of a lifetime smoker. "We were on-again off-again for about ten years."

"I didn't really know him at all," said Roxanne. "My fiancé, Martin, knew him, which is why I'm here. Only Martin disappeared an hour ago to smoke a cigarette, so now I'm here alone."

Cadence had her eyes on Janine.

"And you were married to him?" she said.

Janine wondered if their relationships with Harlin had overlapped.

"It was a long time ago."

"You're the only ex-wife who showed up," said Roxanne.

"All the rest are suing him," said Cadence, and let out a short, raspy laugh. It was a genuine sound, and Janine felt a twinge of jealousy. Harlin would have liked a woman with a raspy laugh. Janine had given up cigarettes when she'd quit hard liquor—and was glad for it—but she had never worn bad habits well. Cadence did.

"Isn't that funny," Cadence said, "the only women who are here for him are his first wife and the one he never married."

"Harlin was a ladykiller," said Jack, adjusting the farmer's cap he wore backwards. "He wasn't meant to be married."

Cadence looked at him in a gentle way, the way you might look at a soldier who's off to fight an unwinnable war. "Oh, honey," she said. "By funny I meant pathetic."

The group began to tell stories about Harlin. They talked about lost jobs, bad luck, the time he almost killed a friend with a broken beer bottle, the house he accidentally set on fire. There were heroic stories, too. Cadence told a story about the time Harlin rode his motorcycle into her bar because it was brand-new and he couldn't wait for her to see it. Rusty brought up the time Harlin took on Jake Grimaldi, who was three times his size and crazy, and might have strangled him if the cops hadn't come and made them both spend the night in jail. Jack remembered when Harlin put on an Easter bonnet to be part of a parade one of the women at the bar put together. Janine told them all about the time Harlin had decided to organize a bus rodeo. "He got a bunch of pylons and set them up on a blacktop, and then he called the paper and left a message on some woman's machine about how he was organizing this big event, with school buses and an obstacle course. He gave her the number of the bar and passed out. When the woman called back, she got the bartender, who said, 'A bus rodeo? Honey, that man's lucky if he can get on a bicycle.'"

Everyone laughed and raised their glasses, and in the moment of silence that followed, Janine, who was getting drunk, remembered her short marriage fondly.

"You know what I loved about Harlin?" she said. "I loved how Harlin could sing. Did you ever hear him? There was so much longing in that voice. He could sound like Hank Williams if he wanted to."

"I think it got him evicted from his last apartment though," Rusty said. "That and a few other things."

"And he was good to his dogs," Janine said, not wanting her warm feelings for her ex-husband to be shut down. "I always trust a man who is good to his dogs."

"I trust a man who is good to his wife," Cadence said. She was looking at Janine when she said this, and Janine heard it as a challenge.

"That's a good reason not to date one that's married," she said.

Cadence looked at her and almost smiled. "I suppose that's true," she said. She ignored the No Smoking signs and lit a cigarette, and Janine wondered what she and Harlin had been like in bed.

Roxanne took out some lipstick and asked Janine if she wanted to see a picture of her daughter. She opened her wallet and showed Janine a picture of a little girl in a pantsuit.

"She's beautiful," said Janine.

"I'm having another one, too, which is why I'm so fat," said Roxanne. She pulled out a photocopy of a sonogram, where a ghostly white shape floated against a dark background. In careful block letters, someone had drawn arrows and written: Eye. Arm. Leg.

"That's beautiful too," Janine said.

Roxanne, who was not drinking, frowned. "You can't see what it looks like yet," she said.

Harlin's sister Angie got up to lead everyone in prayer over the food. Roxanne excused herself to go speak to her fiancé, who was talking to a girl with a nose ring.

"They'll last about six months," said Jack.

"Maybe a year," said Cadence, shaking her head.

Harlin's cousin Earl, long-limbed and round-cheeked, pounded on a cup with his jackknife. He stood up and adjusted his neck brace.

"There was a lot you could say about Harlin," Earl said. "You could say sometimes he went too far, and you could say sometimes he did too much. But Harlin was responsible for the mood in any bar. If he was drinking and the drinking was good, he could light up a place."

The guests nodded. "Harlin was the kind of guy who would give you the shirt off his back," Earl went on, adding that he was also the kind of guy who would rip the shirt off the back of someone who insulted one of his friends. In fact, he had, and Earl told a story about that too.

"But that's not how Harlin wanted to be remembered," Earl said. "He wanted to be remembered as a gentle man. It's not easy, since we all know he had a violent nature." At this, everyone laughed and raised their glasses.

"But there was something in Harlin that always made you want to help him," Earl said. "You couldn't not forgive the man. He had this kindness, a sort of wisdom. Harlin always knew what was eating you whether you told him or not."

Janine took a sip of beer from the can Jack had brought her. She considered the times she had forgiven Harlin: for the other women, the coke binge(s), the things he forgot (her birthday, his car payments). No man had made her as angry as Harlin did, but no one could apologize the way he did either. "I'm so sorry," he'd said, after she caught him groping Linda Hartley in the alley behind Lucy's. "It's just that she reminded me of you, and you had disappeared." That bastard, she thought now. The worst thing about him was that he meant it.

In his later years, Earl was saying, Harlin had reined in his temper. "It was Harlin who tried to teach Martin Pugliese not to pick fights. It was Harlin," he added, who talked to Angie's boy when he went through a bad time and threatened to poison his father."

"Earl!" Angie hissed, but Earl went on.

"The point is," he said, "he was a good man and a free spirit, and that is worth toasting."

Janine raised her cup.

"What about how he stole his ex-wife's money?" said Cadence.

Janine looked at her. "I'm not talking about you," Cadence said, not unkindly. "I'm talking about his most recent ex-wife."

Jack rolled his eyes. "Here we go."

"You know why she sued him?" She was looking at Janine. "He took all her money to start a petting zoo out at his father's broken-down house. There was nothing out there but a few mean dogs, a goat, and some ducks."

Janine wondered if Cadence were drunk. She figured she was, since Janine herself was quite drunk and Cadence was a much thinner woman. But who wouldn't be upset by the loss of a man she'd loved enough to throw out and take back for ten years?

"A child would get mange or rabies out at a place like that," Cadence said.

"He was an entrepreneur," said Jack. "A free spirit."

"It's a lot easier to be a free spirit when someone else is cleaning up the mess," said Cadence. She got up to go sit with Cyrus, the last living male Wilder, who was threatening to punch his brother-in-law in the eye.

"She's not bad-looking for an older lady," Rusty said.

Jack shrugged and pulled out his wallet.

"You want to see a picture of my kid?" he said to Janine. He showed her a snapshot of a tiny blond boy with huge cheeks and messy hair.

"We were down in Florida then," he said.

"What were you doing in Florida?" Janine asked. The fact that he had traveled surprised her. Jack, with his sullen posture and sly face struck her as the kind of guy who got up every day, went to his job washing dishes or pumping gas, got wasted at night and drove around with his friends. He looked like the kind of guy who never left town, didn't even want to, because there were too many jerk-offs in the world, and he had enough to deal with in his own county.

"My wife wanted us to live near her family," he said. Harlin's sister Angie rushed past their table with a pan of baked beans, while her husband stood in the corner, looking for someone to talk to. "But I got drunk and got into a fistfight with her dad and now we're back here."

Angie's husband settled on Earl, who had been telling off-color jokes about priests and now wanted to arm-wrestle Stewart Levine.

Rusty had picked up a pen and was drawing on Roxanne's sonogram. "I can't fight when I'm drunk," he said. "I get too mean. I'm a little guy, but I can drink about a case, and then when I'm smoking pot on top of that . . . ." He shrugged as if to say who knew what would happen.

"Yeah, he drinks like that and then he gets his second wind," said Jack, picking at some facial hair that was growing in no particular order on his chin.

"I don't even know what I do," Rusty said. "My wife gets mad at me."

"I can understand that," Janine said. "If I was your wife, I would get mad at you."

"But you have a nice personality," Rusty said. "She doesn't. She's mean."

"She's vindictive," Jack said.

"Yeah," said Rusty. "But I love her. We're about to have a little baby."

"You love your wife," said Jack, "but you aren't in love with her."

"No, I'm in love with her," Rusty said. "I knew we'd have problems, that's why I married her right away. You never know, things might work out." He looked at Janine as if asking her permission to have this hope.

"They might," she said, granting it. Then she said, "I married Harlin because I knew we'd have problems." She said this because she wanted to make Rusty feel less alone, but as she spoke, she realized that it was true. She'd known right away that it wouldn't last. She could see the trouble with Harlin before it started happening, the promises he'd never be able to keep, the way his eyes got restless when it was five and he hadn't had a drink yet, how it was never his fault when he got in trouble at work. Even at age nineteen, Janine, who was a practical woman, knew this was no good. But the night he'd proposed, Harlin had taken her ordinary face in his hands and said, "I could never get tired of looking at you." She knew that he would, that she was not beautiful in that way, and that he was drunk enough that he might not even remember this the next morning. But to be looked at like that. If I give this up now, she'd thought, will anyone ever look at me this way again? So she'd married him, to keep that for a little while.

"It didn't work though," she said now.

"It didn't really work for me either," said Rusty. "I still love her though. We'll see when the baby comes. She's my first wife, and I'm her first husband, and I want to do right by her. I'm paying child support no matter what."

Stewart Levine got up and straightened the lapels on his corduroy suit. He said Harlin hadn't lost his spirit, even when he was in the hospital. He'd thanked God for the nurses, and even got one of them to slip him some Jack Daniel's before he died.

At their table, Jack told Janine that Harlin hadn't had any spirit at all. He was just lying there, stupidly, pissing in a bag, and it was Stewart who thanked God for the nurses, one redhead in particular, and that was the main reason he kept going over there to visit Harlin. In fact, it was Stewart who brought in the Jack Daniel's "for Harlin," even though everyone knew Harlin drank gin. Then Stewart drank the JD himself until he asked the redheaded nurse if she would come to his house in that uniform and was forced to leave.

Rusty had pulled his chair a little closer to Janine and was still talking about his wife. "I bought her a thousand-dollar ring and everything," he said. "But she wore it on a trampoline and the prongs got bent and the diamond won't stay in. I don't know. I have to find another girl because she's all I think about and I can't be thinking about that anymore." He smiled helplessly. Janine noticed that one of his front teeth was broken, which made him look cunning from a certain angle.

"You know? I just need someone to be with. I'd cook, I'd wash dishes."

"Trey, the man I live with, is a great cook," said Janine, figuring it was time to mention her boyfriend. It was a tactic she used to use in her drinking days, when men complained hungrily to her about their wives or ex-girlfriends. Sometimes it worked, other times it made her more attractive. "He washes dishes and he picks up. I feel guilty about it sometimes because I'm such a slob."

"You know what you can do," Jack said. "If you have a glass of something, pick it up and take it with you next time you go into the kitchen."

"Don't leave stuff behind the bathroom door," said Rusty.

"Oh, I fucking hate that," said Jack.

"Really?" said Janine. "I always do that. I go in, take my clothes off, take a shower, and then go into the bedroom to get dressed. Who cares about the clothes behind the door?" It occurred to her that maybe she shouldn't be talking about taking her clothes off to two men half her age at Harlin's funeral. But then she decided that, no, that was exactly what she should be doing at Harlin's funeral.

"Take your clothes with you," Jack was saying.

"Or put them in a hamper," Rusty said.

"You can make a chore list," said Jack.

The crowd of mourners had finished eating and had begun to relax, stretching arms across the backs of chairs, loosening belts and ties. Jack got up to get some more beer and Rusty got up to go the bathroom. Janine sat by herself, enjoying a little solitude in the crowded room. She looked at the people around her—Cyrus in his one fine suit, Earl trying to look over his neck brace and down Angie Wilder's dress. Angie almost letting him. Roxanne's fiancé swearing he didn't do a thing. It was as if Harlin were everywhere, in every man in the room. And then it seemed as if every woman were some version of her, or what she might have been if she'd stayed. She missed Harlin terribly then, as much as she missed herself as a younger woman. A sweet melancholy passed through her—a mixture of grief, longing and love that felt like homesickness.

Yet it was getting later, and the party was starting to turn. Someone had written the word "penis" on Roxanne's sonogram and drawn an arrow to what looked like the baby's head. Rusty and Jack came back to the table reeking of smoke, and Rusty started complaining about no-smoking laws. Cadence was still on Cyrus's lap, and Jack said Cadence would probably end up that night with Cyrus, Harlin's brother—once a slut, always a slut.

"She's good-looking for an older lady, though," Rusty said.

"You said that already," Jack said. He looked bored and asked Janine if she wanted to see his tattoos. Without waiting for an answer, he pulled up his shirt. Inside an uneven circle, a crucifix, halfway filled in, took up most of his chest. "I was going to get one of those Chinese ying-yangs on my stomach," he said. "But I figured I'm going to grow old and get all fat and it would stretch out."

Rusty pulled up his shirtsleeve to show off what looked like fish scales or chain mail covering his forearm. Then he showed her more of the same design on his calf. Each tattoo looked homemade, as if Rusty had stabbed himself a hundred thousand times with a Bic pen.

"It's armor," he said. "I got the idea from that video game Doom."

"Yeah," said Jack. "All he does is sit at home drawing medieval shit." He absentmindedly picked at a scab on his arm. "Show her the best one."

Rusty unbuttoned his shirt and revealed his finest tattoo. It was the same design, but this time it took up half his chest. When Janine saw it, she gasped, not because the tattoo was horrifying, which it was, but because through its center, down the middle of Rusty's torso, ran a vertical red scar, long and thick as a kitchen knife.

The scar was so angry, stuck in the middle of that scaly, blue web, that Janine felt a wave of sadness just looking at it. "Oh, Rusty," she said. "What happened to you?"

Rusty looked down at his chest as if trying to figure out whether she was talking about the scar or the tattoo. "Someone beat me up when I was a baby," he said.

Janine's head was beginning to swim.

"No one knows who did it," said Jack. "Or if they do they're not saying. All they know is that someone dropped him off all cut up and bloody at St. Anthony's."

"I had so many broken bones they had to cut me open," Rusty said. "The orderly had to hold my heart in his hands and pump it himself to keep me alive."

Janine put her hand on Rusty's cheek. "St. Anthony's is a mental institution, not a hospital," she said. She knew the place well; she had done a rotation there in nursing school. It was a lonesome, rambling brick building with hard lighting and sprawling grounds that had once housed fruit trees and rich gardens. This fucking town, she thought. Who would think a loony bin would be a good place for a baby? And who would beat a child like that? She knew from her work that it could be any number of desperate people, too trapped by their own rage and bitterness to know what else to do. Still, a baby. An infant. There should be a limit on what people could do.

She took her hand away, and Rusty looked at his beer. "I'm not real proud of my tattoos," he said. "I was only sixteen when I got most of them."

Harlin's brother Cyrus came over and said he was going to be out drinking that night until he ran out of money. "Then," he said, "I am going to find some more money, so I can put it on the horses."

Jack though that sounded like a good idea and left without saying goodbye. Janine decided it was time to go too. She gathered up her purse and sweater and was about to leave, when without looking up from the beer he was drinking Rusty said, "Harlin was the guy who brought me to the mental hospital that night."

Janine stopped.

"I don't know that much about it," he said, looking at her now. "He was living downstairs from us then, and I guess my birth mother showed up at his door and asked him to get me out of the house."

Janine sat back down. She saw the whole thing then: A frantic woman showing up at Harlin's door, Harlin, saddened and annoyed by the shit he had to deal with agreeing to take care of her baby. She saw Harlin wrapping Rusty in one of the ratty blankets he kept in the back of his truck and speeding to the hospital without a car seat. She imagined that baby, lying in the front seat or across Harlin's lap, unable to cry without breaking something else, and her ex-husband trying to soothe him by singing some old country song about loneliness or bad women. Then she saw Harlin pass the hospital because he was probably drunk and wouldn't want to answer any questions, and driving to St. Anthony's, where he probably knew someone who worked there. It was so typical, she thought, of that man to do the right thing and rescue a child, but then end up missing the hospital and drop the baby off at an insane asylum.

"It's funny," Rusty said. "He saved me at the beginning of my life, and now here I am at his funeral. Makes you wonder about things."

"I guess," Janine said. In the corner, Roxanne was talking to her fiancé, who was looking past her head and off into the distance as if he'd already heard what she was saying a thousand times. Janine turned back to Rusty and started to laugh. "Harlin," she said. "Jesus

Christ. You're lucky he didn't drop you off at a bowling alley."

Rusty laughed too, and then asked Janine if she wanted to come out for a drink, but Janine had had enough for one day.

"Maybe another time," she said.

"You're not bad-looking for an older lady," Rusty said. "If things don't work out with your old man, you should call me up.

Outside, Janine stood, listening to the night sounds of the place she grew up in. It was an early fall night, the kind that Harlin had always loved, when there was a bite to the air that stirred things up--people, livestock, the wind. She thought about her ex-husband, and then she thought about Rusty starting his life with his heart in someone else's hand. She thought of all the hope he had for his doomed marriage and his unborn baby. That was what had always gotten her about Harlin, his relentless hope. It was what kept him from being a bad man, and part of what made him a stupid one. She thought about Cadence, Harlin's ex-girlfriend, and how she loved and hated him still.

Down the street she could see the mourners staggering out of the lodge, two or three at a time, some singing; one woman, Cadence, she guessed, crying. It was a beautiful, romantic night, and this made Janine nostalgic for Harlin again. "Say what you will about drunks," she said out loud to the Masonic Lodge. "But no one can love you the way they can."

She started to walk to her truck but knew she wasn't quite ready to drive the forty-five minutes back to her house. So instead she walked to the Royal Court Inn, where she and Harlin had stayed one night years ago when they were too drunk to drive anywhere. She booked a room, and when she got inside, put her purse down on the bed and took off her panty hose. She was still thinking about Harlin as she slipped her underwear off under her skirt and put on some lipstick. Then she picked up the phone and called Lanford, who she knew was at home, drinking and waiting, if not for her, then for something or someone. "Lanford," she said when he answered. "It's me."

"Janine," Lanford said. "How are you holding up?"

"Good," she said. "Fine. Drunk."

In the pause that followed, she could hear a cat yowling somewhere in Lanford's house.

"Should I come over?" he said.

"I think that would be best," she said. She gave him her room number and hung up.

Janine turned off the lights in the room and lit a cigarette. As she sat waiting for Lanford, she drank a bourbon in Harlin's honor. She thought about how he taught her to dance, and to talk dirty, and how long it had been since she had had good, sloppy, drunken sex like the kind she was about to have. She thanked Harlin for all that as she sat there smoking, a habit she'd given up long ago but still loved. He was her first husband, and she was his first wife, and she wanted to do right by him.

The Ecotone Interview

A longtime Coloradan, Reg Saner first saw mountains during military service when he was sent to Big Delta, Alaska, for alpine and arctic survival training. After combat duty as an infantry platoon leader in the Korean war, he studied renaissance culture at the University of Illinois and as a Fulbright scholar in Florence, Italy, at the Universitá degli Studi. Among other honors, his previous writings, all set in the American West, have won several national prizes, including the first Walt Whitman Award as conferred by the Academy of American Poets and the Copernicus Society of America. His second book was a National Poetry Series "Open Competition" winner, selected by Derek Walcott, later a Nobel laureate. Saner has won an NEA fellowship, the Creede Repertory Theater Award, the State of Colorado Governor's Award, and the Wallace Stegner Award conferred by the Center of the American West. His nonfiction books include a recent omnibus edition of *The Four-Cornered Falcon: Essays on the Interior West* and *The Natural Scene* (Kodansha America Inc., 1994) and *Reaching Keet Seel: Ruin's Echo & the Anasazi* (University of Utah Press, 1998). In spring 2005 the Center for American Places published *The Dawn Collector: On My Way to the Natural World*. Saner's prose and poetry have appeared in more than fifty anthologies.

with Reg Saner
David Gessner

David Gessner: I don't know of a contemporary essay I admire more than "Technically Sweet." It is common enough to create an essay with two or three subject threads, but in "Sweet" you weave at least six distinct themes. Within the essay you discuss the purely technical pleasure that Oppenheimer and others took in building the atomic bomb. Did you take some technical pleasure in creating this essay? Can you describe how you built it? Was there a sense of challenge? Of play?

Reg Saner: Yes, the challenge was deliberate enough, though the parallel never occurred to me. I'd already written quite a few essays using straight-ahead, linear sequence. They found takers without much trouble, but I remember telling myself, "You'll never improve if you don't try something you're not sure you can do."

In poetry the sestina form had always interested me, though not enough to write them. They're too much like playing the piano with the backs of your fingers. The instant a reader sees, "Oh, this is a sestina," poetry gets upstaged by the parlor trick of recurrent line-endings. My material for "Technically Sweet" embodied a half-dozen themes, so I thought, "It's true, all but a handful of sestinas tend to become a mere juggling act, but in a long prose piece the scheme wouldn't be nearly so visible. Since I've got themes enough, maybe I can bring it off."

I guess you're right about challenge. Ending with an essay instead of a mess was technically sweet.

Gessner: I remember something you said during a talk in Colorado two summers ago: "I haven't been changed one fraction as much by writing poetry as by my creative nonfiction. Or by all my other learning it seems . . . ." You irked a couple of poets in the audience, but the idea stuck with me. That by throwing yourself into your essays, by doing the work of learning and observing they required, you were expanding, even re-creating, yourself.

Saner: Well, irking poets isn't hard to do. Kenneth Rexroth once said, "Ninety-eight percent of the worst people I've ever known have been poets." Don't their first wives almost always divorce them? I'm the only one-wife poet I know. Marcia Southwick was having dinner with my wife, Anne, and me out on our patio shortly after she and Larry Levis split, and I clearly recall her murmuring, half to herself, "Never again a poet."

Am I going to get mail?

As someone who published four collections of poetry, three of which won national prizes, I didn't dream nonfiction would teach me incomparably more than my work in verse. No comparison. That in itself was quite a discovery. Through nonfiction I'm much closer to the person I'd like to be. Which has absolutely nothing to do with ego, just me as a talking animal among billions. As to the poetic mode, only the critically naïve would say it has to happen in verse. People often tell me this or that passage in my prose is "poetic." Well, yeah, but not accidentally. The very best prose often is, though never the poesy kind. Most so-called lyric prose is neither one nor the other. The opening verses of Genesis are great poetry by not being what Frost snidely called "very poetickal."

Gessner: You once wrote to me about "God in all his weasly disguises." Dogma seems to be one of your great enemies, and you have written about being offended by "pat answers and no questions." On the other hand, in *The Dawn Collector,* you describe yourself as "incorrigibly religious." Can you describe your own "mystery religion" and how it differs from what passes for religion today?

Saner: Nobody can say I haven't given God every chance to prove himself. Having spent years being sermonized and gazing at stained-glass fables way over my head, I'm qualified to agree with Woody Allen: "If there is one, he's a terrific underachiever." All through grade school and high school I was taught by Dominican nuns in black wimples over ankle-length white linen. I adored them then and still do. My Catholic college added four years of priests. In fact, during my early teens I wanted to become the first priest on Mars, thinking if there were Martians, the harvest would be wonderful. Gradually I came far enough out of Plato's cave to realize that God was the worst idea humans ever had.

Christians have often behaved worse than Murder Incorporated. In Rouen I stood on the spot where *la pucelle,* Joan of Arc, was burnt alive. Having lived in Florence I've also passed, hundreds of times, the exact spot in the Piazza della Signoria where Savonarola was torched. Ditto for Rome's Campo dei Fiori, where the Inquisition set fire to a stark-naked Giordano Bruno.

To be religious in my sense is to feel and act on your relation to all other talking animals, asteroids, DNA, coyotes, cottonwoods, bluebirds, grasses, supernovae, yellow-bellied marmots, microbes, in short, all that is. Earth being the only heaven we'll ever have, we should as a species stop turning it into a hell. That's heretical but hardly radical.

Gessner: At one point in *Reaching Keet Seel* you mention the "whimsical" phrase "the pleasure of where." This seems to describe much of your life and work. Can you describe the ways that "where" has impacted your work?

Saner: Whereness? Well, yes, for me life is far more a question of place than of people. Even so, I can't imagine a worse fate than to own the whole world and be the only one in it. It's just that the natural world happens to surprise me far more often than humans ever do. We differ only in what we reveal. What we conceal is identical.

Gessner: I can't think of a greater, wilder pleasure than hiking though the desert and coming unexpectedly upon an Anasazi dwelling. Can you describe what the Anasazi have meant to you as a writer? What I mean is that their history fits so perfectly with so many of your themes that if they didn't exist, you'd have to invent them. They dovetail with your love of ruins; they prove the impermanence and smallness of humans; they work as metaphor as well as being fascinating in themselves. Can you describe some of the pleasures of uncovering and exploring their gone lives?

Saner: Of course I did describe it, pretty much throughout *Reaching Keet Seel.* The seed of that book was a question: "Why do I love visiting these Anasazi ruins?" By then I'd pondered them in Utah, Arizona, New Mexico, and Colorado. Their fusion with Southwestern settings exerts an almost narcotic allure. Then there's scale. The imperial size of a Roman ruin makes it a version of Shelley's "Ozymandias," whereas an Anasazi site is our own size, each village less wide than a voice. You feel an intimate pathos in the scattered potsherds, corn cobs, empty rooms. Rome was blood and iron, while the Anasazi were hoes and planting sticks—for their corn, beans, and squash. Coming across even so little as one of their granaries, you marvel at their imprints in the adobe—thumbs and fingers busy with wall building eight centuries ago—but still so real you almost overhear their voices.

Gessner: You have written that there are times that overly rigorous scientific writing can taste like "canned spinach." At the same time a degree of rigor marks your work in contrast to some "softer" and more personal essayists. "My walks are my research," you've said. But your research is your research, too. Can you talk about the process of building some of your long essays? How do research and personal experience meld?

Saner: For "Technically Sweet" I read eighteen books and traveled about 1,500 miles, interviewed people, then used a small fraction of what was in my database. Even so, any reader curious about the ironic role played by the beauty of northern New Mexico in making the A-bomb—especially Oppenheimer's relation to New Mexico—will get lots of factuality without losing the big picture.

In working up a topic I make hundreds of notes, so as to know what I'm talking about, and probably use less than ten percent. My study is crammed with card files. Your own fieldwork for *Return of the Osprey* must have generated tons more info than you ended up using. Theodore Roethke was talking about poetry when he said, "Ah, cutting. The great art," equally true in prose. Like John Ashbery's witty definition of poetry as "this leaving-out business."

Right now I've fifty-seven pages of a short book I'm doing, with another thirty pages of cut wordage. Being a frugal sort of spendthrift, I always save it, hoping I might be able to use it elsewhere. I rarely do. Maybe the best writing advice ever given is a statement by Ernest Hemingway: "One judges the quality of a story by the quality of the writing that was cut out of it." If a beginner pasted that in his hat he'd be in good shape.

Gessner: "Mountains are time we can see," you wrote. Can you tell us a little about your background? Growing up in the Midwest and moving to the Front Range. And also coming out of the army and deciding to become a poet. . . .

Saner: Growing up in downstate Illinois, I couldn't see the world. Fence lines and furrows humanized the land, made it rational. Ancient history was no deeper than the chert arrowheads my uncle Frank turned up with his plow. In Boulder my house sits on the edge of open space in full view of massive upthrusts of reddish sandstone laid down some 300 million years ago. Within walking distance, two peaks rise some 2,600 feet above our roof. Gone time fascinates me, and the Colorado I love looks like time petrified, Darwin's "enormous quantities of time." My house is partly landscaped with boulders older than Rome. Older than civilization. For that matter, older than man. Wonderful hunks of time turned to stone.

I remember first stepping outside the station in Rome and almost fainting with delight at dramatically floodlit scraps of its ancient Servian Wall. Milton wrote about an era when "all our fathers worshiped stocks and stones." I still worship old trees, old stones. With a heavy-duty wheelbarrow and a wrecking bar I've pried up enough red rock for trundling into my yard to make a state park back in Illinois.

Funny, I never decided to become a poet, just admired poetry so much I tried writing it.

But poets are few and far between. That's why if I can avoid it I don't call myself one—except when side-stepping the word would be silly. In poems and prose my one subject is simply my sense of the world. Various topics angle toward it differently—like spokes of a bicycle wheel—toward that hub. In my mountain poems, mountains are only the apparent subject. Same with prose on Southwestern desert, the Grand Canyon, and so on. The true subject is always some sort of take on the marginality of humans in a world they inhabit barely long enough to look around.

Gessner: Yes, a central insight of yours, repeated in various ways, is just how small and relatively insignificant we human beings are. Many of us repeat this, but you seem to truly *feel* it. Does part of this spring from spending so much time thinking about the universe in a larger sense—the cosmos? And is that what you are getting at in "Lone Skier in Glacier Gorge"? Or is that moment slightly different, a more unique and particular vision?

Saner: Being alive is the one strangest thing that can possibly happen. Nothing else comes close. Compared to the total of cosmic matter lacking consciousness, we humans might as well be called "infinitesimals." Because that's where we are and how it is. As Emily Dickinson says, "I'm nobody! Who are you? / Are you—Nobody—Too?" Being one of Euclid's geometric points, location but no magnitude, doesn't depress me. It's an effect of my jaw-dropping awe at all we belong to. There's sheer wonder in a Hubble deep-space photo revealing galaxies thick as snow where the naked eye sees nothing but the midnight of empty sky. I love Plato's claim that wonder is the beginning of philosophy, maybe because wonder's my weakness. I enthuse and get amazed all over the place. My mother was like that. She was a great appreciator.

Catholicism gave me a daily sense of living in two worlds at once, terrestrial and celestial. I still live there, but it's all far more mysterious without the God hypothesis. When it comes to outer space, we're in it, and to all the other inhabited planets we're ETs. Again, that's how it is because everything local is cosmic, even a wife's pink panties.

Gessner: A pressing question for many of us is how to reconcile our love of this world with a greater pessimism about what we are doing to the planet. (And I do mean *we*, not *them*—some evil other like "developers"—since I use as much gasoline as the next guy.) Can you offer any insight into reconciling these feelings?

Saner: It's sorry but true that global warming and peak oil come from human spawn overrunning the earth. Worse yet, we're a weed species whose evolutionary development took a bloody turn, so we live on a ship of fools, many of them murderous. Even sorrier to say, the slow holocaust we inflicted on Native Americans is merely an instance.

So according to me, the Buddhists have it right about changing the world: "Start with yourself." As a low-impact environmentalist, however, I've plenty of room for improvement. Still, Anne and I have two offspring only. We recycle and try to buy green products. Our Volvo wagon is eighteen years old, with less than 50,000 miles on it, and mile-

61

age on my twelve-year-old pickup is exactly half the national average. I bicycle and walk where feasible, and use a push mower powered by granola. As to the planet's future, it's a real downer to realize the nitty-gritty is filthy lucre. As a character in Shakespeare says, "And oft 'tis seen the wicked prize itself / buys out the law." In another play, much the same: "Plate sin with gold, / And the strong lance of justice hurtless breaks; / Arm it in rags, a pygmy's straw does pierce it." I wish pessimistic optimism weren't the best I can do, but that's the situation. Bad guys make megabucks out of raping nature, absolutely looting it, whereas in trying to stop them the good guys don't make one dime.

Gessner: In our first issue Ann Zwinger described her favorite ecotone. Any particular local ecotone that fascinates you? Does the mesa out your backdoor qualify? The Front Range itself?

Saner: On my mesa-walk near our house there's a particular bend in the trail, some five hundred feet above my house. To my right rises a steep couloir with windfallen trunks across talus. Above its chute of tumbled stone rise sandstone sheernesses way overhead, about nine hundred feet higher. Then just to my left there's a continuation of the talus down a steep ravine, also timbered deep evergreen by handsome Douglas fir and ponderosa pine. It's a sort of "Wow!" point. Utterly untouched wilderness a thirty-minute walk from my door.

    Summer evenings, I may sit atop a huge lion-colored slab, munching my sandwich and sipping from a half-pint canteen of white wine while watching Steller's jays, towhees, and mauve clouds reflecting the light's changes. Wildflowers abound. A favorite is horsemint, or bergamot, with lavender blossoms plump as muffins, and maybe a nectar-sipping moth flicking its proboscis. The trail passes through many fine places, but that particular spot always causes the Midwesterner in me to feel, "This is what I wanted."

Gessner: How many days a year do you collect dawn?

Saner: As I explain in *The Dawn Collector*, to make sunrise a duty would ruin everything, so I'm careful to go out only when I want to. Today the sun rose at 5:50, in clear air. I felt good, so up the mesa I went. Me and the mule deer—and my silly familiars, the magpies. As you know,

Boulder has lots of sunny days. I suppose I go out for dawn maybe two hundred times a year, and really feel my luck in living where I can not only see clear to the horizon, but also have a life with that kind of freedom.

So dawn's gold-and-cobalt sky's a blessing all right, but its source is blind fire. Occasionally, before the solar sphere clears the horizon, I'll say a poem, Blake, Dickinson, Hopkins, though I couldn't tell you why. Just do. The deer don't seem to mind. For that matter, I like saying a poem or two aloud when I walk. I'm a word person, and a good poem feels good to say.

As to my "thing" about dawn, Pee Wee Russell, a jazz clarinetist, defended his maverick style by declaring, "The note I blow may be the wrong note for anyone else, but it's the right note for me."

Lone Skier in Glacier George
Reg Saner

All afternoon blown snow has screamed
off the summits into sky's high-altitude
cobalt. Even now as the sun dips westerly
and ice crags burn gold at the edges
those snow-shapes keep hurling up,
dervishing so wildly away
over iron peaks of the headwall
I pause, ski pole in each mittened hand
and lean forward, spellbound.

Worlds beyond my own little whiff
of existence, and these pitiful schemes
we believe we believe in, I'm held
by more than just whirlwind crystals
ripped from escarpments of granite.
Within white fire's endless wheel
Apparitional I see myself done for, shot
with my own blood . . . by an immense
incandescence bound to annihilate me
and all it makes, as it must, to be
what it is. A radiance so beyond knowable
I can't wish it otherwise. And can't want to.

Then, unbidden as it came, the revelation
wanes, leaving the one true thing
tremendously gone
and our entire, ingenious planet,
a blown snowflake.

Returned, I'm once more in a deep glacial valley
filling to the brim with tinted shadow.
The great-hearted, snow-loaded fir,
the hugely stupid boulders

Reg Saner

I love, the dear wind-haggard spruce,
wind-flustered ravens.

All of us, one sky-lit and empty blue.

Fiat Lux
Reg Saner

Let givers of flying lessons
whose answers for famine
and genocide come easy
as ventriloquism
learn someday to forego
those pious voices thrown
as if from beyond the stars,
and so make way for a time and life
when this planet celestial
and earthly sees even the least
of its children grow into beliefs
humane enough
with sky stories true enough
to live this one.

Let then the sun's own person
hovering above
the lowliest rose that ever was
declare all petals and pollen
the mother of god.

Companionable
Reg Saner

Hours alone on big granite open him
to suggestion. Hears things. A horsefly's
buzz grows conversational, human.
A cascade's far-off-ness mimics the rise
and fall in syllables, windblown. From snow
couloirs blue enough, a caw's inflection
may float to his ear like talk—as do just now
a couple of ravens winging high above tarns
late October has frozen below them.

He sees autumn sun edging them
and him and every roundabout summit
in rust, and loves it. And loves as always
their veers far apart, then their long glides
that tilt and flirt like affection, as they sidle
and close. Those casual maneuvers
mated ravens all use.

So keeps them in view
till their chatty squawk and reply
has flown into stillness miles and miles wide
leaving no sound whatever . . . except
a third animal's breathing. Surprised
how truly their passage, while it lasted,
made him companionable too.

eight paintings
JOAN SNYDER

Born April 16, 1940 in Highland Park, New Jersey, Joan Snyder received her AB from Douglass College in New Brunswick, New Jersey (1962) and an MFA from Rutgers University (1966), also in New Brunswick. She was the recipient of a National Endowment for the Arts fellowship (1974) and a John Simon Guggenheim Memorial fellowship (1983).

Snyder's entrance into the art world began with a series of "Stroke" paintings which shaped her first solo shows in New York City and San Francisco and were selected for the Whitney Annual 1972, the 1973 Whitney Biennial and the Corcoran 1975 Biennial. In 1978, the Neuberger Museum in Purchase, New York, presented a solo exhibition of her work. Since then, her paintings have been shown in numerous gallery and museum exhibitions. They are also included in major museum, corporate, and private collections.

In 2005 the Jewish Museum in New York City presented a thirty-five-year survey of her work, which then traveled to the Danforth Museum in Framingham, Massachusetts. Abrams Books published a monograph, *Joan Snyder*, with an introduction by Norman Kleeblatt and essays by Hayden Herrera and Jenni Sorkin in conjunction with this touring exhibition. Other recent museum exhibitions include solo shows at the Allentown Art Museum (1993), tthe Rose Art Museum, the Parrish Art Museum (1994), and the Brooklyn Museum of Art (1998).

Although Snyder's paintings are often placed under various art-movement umbrellas—abstract expressionism, neo-expressionism, feminist art—the changing nature of her work, with its combination of personal iconography, female imagery, aggressive brushstroke, and accomplished formalism, has kept her steadily untagged.

Snyder lives in Brooklyn and Woodstock, New York.

All the Things

Late Summer Pond

Alizarin and Ice

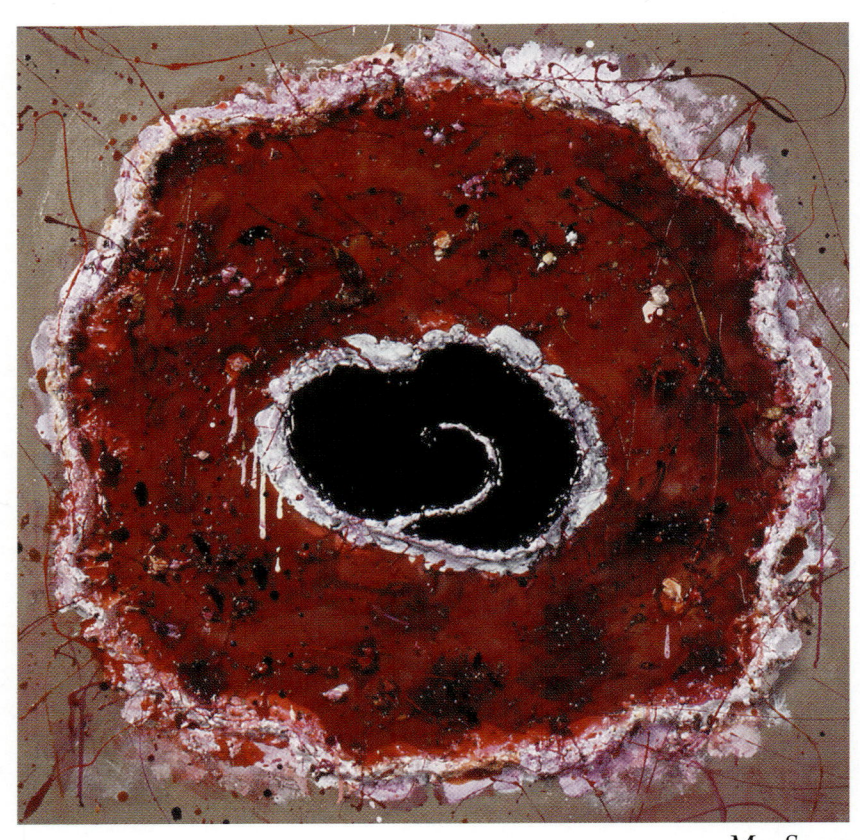

My Song

Night

Baby Blue Yonder

Color/Field

Summer Pond

Ghosts in the Woodshed
Katie Fallon

The sun never hit our house on the ridge. Pine trees surrounded it on three sides, their branches hugging its dirty-white walls. The wind that whipped down the mountain shook needles and cones onto our roof and into the rusted gutters. Moss crawled up the cinderblock foundation. Fingers of cool, green mold wrapped around the unfinished basement walls. Ivy spilled down the steep hill from the house, tangling around the stones of the driveway's retaining wall. Ghosts were everywhere—between the perfectly straight lines of apple trees, beneath the peach and pear trees, ensnared in the gooseberry bushes and the grapevines twisting up rotted wooden posts.

My husband, Jesse, and I did not actually own this property—we rented it from a veterinarian friend of ours—but we had plans for it. A small barn stood about a hundred feet from the house, and we hoped to convert it into a rehabilitation area for injured and orphaned birds. Peach trees lined the grassy path that led from our house to the barn; tiger swallow tail butterflies and goldfinches crowded the high purple thistles along the path's edge. The overgrown remains of another nearby shed, this one brick with no roof, were barely noticeable, buried in a thick patch of deer tongue and rosebushes. The path ended at the barn, which was a perfectly square structure, its dimensions about thirty feet by thirty feet, its base several rows of stacked cinderblocks. The walls and roof were scalloped sheet metal. The side facing the house gaped like a garage without a door. The vines that tangled around the cinderblocks bordering the open front threatened to spill the blocks and wreck the barn.

The owner of the property told us she had let a homeless man live in the barn, but he disappeared. "Disappeared?" I asked. "Well, left without letting me know," she corrected. Apparently the man, Carl, was a woodworker, and his presence was everywhere. Odds and ends were piled to the barn's ceiling. At first, it all looked like junk: blue Maxwell

House coffee cans filled with Carl's cigarette butts, a small wooden chair with three legs, a twisted metal ladder from a pool or boat. In the center of the room, a rusted wheelbarrow lay on its side, spilling chunks of coal across the concrete floor. In one corner sat a TV missing its screen. These were all the ghosts of dreams, important at one time, invested in. What accident caused the boat's ladder to twist like that? What child once sat in the broken chair?

The room was also filled with lumber of various shapes, sizes, textures, and degrees of decay. Some of the boards looked like they'd been purchased yesterday, while others were coated in peeling paint and sported twisted, rusty nails. There were thin strips of molding, two-by-fours, and sheets of particle board, as well as chunks of expensive-looking cedar. Rolls of insulation were stacked along the back wall of the room, still in their brown wrappers. In a back corner loomed a thing that looked like a busted water heater. Above all this, packed-mud wasp and hornet nests clung to rafters. Three bird nests bunched in high corners made by support beams. We had been discouraged. Someone had lived here? Where?

The barn was bisected by a particle-board wall. The door that led to the other "room" seemed out of place amid all the chaos—it was expertly made of slanted wood planks and it had an elaborate lock. To open the door, a wooden handle had to be turned, almost spun, a half-circle. This would move the wooden bolt from the latch and allow the door to swing open. The other room was more livable, but only slightly. The front of the room, the side that faced our house, was closed in by the corrugated sheet metal, but the back was partially open to the outdoors. A door frame with a Plexiglas pane lay flat on the grass beyond the opening. This unfinished door didn't have hinges.

This other room had clearly been Carl's woodshed and primary living space. A ledge ran around the inside of the wall; stacked on it were Mason jars filled with nuts, bolts, nails, screws, and hinges. Scraps of sandpaper and wood shavings cluttered the concrete floor. A curl of sloughed snakeskin twisted in a corner. Mouse droppings were scattered everywhere like black rice. Shelves along one wall held piles of mail with Carl's name on the labels; under his name, "The Woodshed" was listed on the second address line. Unfinished projects collected dust—a paper towel holder, a mirror, a creepy deer head carved into the top of a large branch, and pencil-sketched plans on the backs of envelopes. On another shelf were three small boxes, each containing 1,000 unsharpened blue pencils. Each pencil had "Monogalia County Police Reserve. Buckle Up For Safety. Say No To Drugs." etched onto it. Our county is *Monongalia*; the police had misspelled it on their pencils, another careful plan gone wrong. Obviously, Carl had meant to seal this room, fit the insulation into the walls, and live there comfortably in a woodworker's paradise. The room even had an old coal stove; its pipe went out of the barn through a roughly cut opening in the sheet metal. Just inside the back wall sat a green plastic chair with a hole cut out of the seat—we assumed this had been Carl's mobile commode.

Just behind the barn, in an overgrown clearing, an empty heating-oil drum, an aluminum cattle gate, some sort of strange incubator, and an ancient hay rake slowly rusted. Thin sumac trunks sprouted from between the twisted wreckage, threatening to hide the discarded machinery forever. Empty cans of paint thinner and wood stain were strewn around the ground, contents having seeped into the earth months or maybe years before. Rotten skids with rotten boards stacked on them were pushed up against the barn. Rusty nails jutted from almost every plank—lockjaw waiting to happen. The tangled clearing was surrounded by wild black raspberries and tall pine trees where indigo buntings and brown thrashers nested.

Taking care of injured birds would not be a new venture for us. Jesse, who hoped to become a veterinarian himself, occasionally brought avian orphans home from the animal hospital where he worked as a technician. We also volunteered at a local raptor rehabilitation center, where for weeks before we moved into the house on the ridge we nursed a screech owl that had been hit by a car; the owl's right humerus had been broken. Fortunately, the bone healed quickly, but the accident had torn a hole in the thin skin that stretched between the bird's body and the wing. The vet stitched it together twice, but both times the owl picked out the stitches. We grew anxious, but during controlled test flights, the bird seemed to fly almost perfectly, even with the hole. So we celebrated moving into our new house by turning it loose back there, behind the barn. I said a prayer, made a wish, and tossed the little owl into the pine trees beyond the overgrown clearing, into a darkening summer evening. I wonder if the wind whistles through the hole in its wing when it flies.

A week after moving to the ridge, we gathered up garbage bags and brooms, called a few willing friends, and took the first steps towards renovating the barn. Dust suspended in the air under the fluorescent light tubes that had miraculously hummed to life with only minimal adjustments to the wiring. We pushed large objects into the overgrown clearing behind the barn, including a set of two cobwebbed sawhorses. Then, we each took a garbage bag and slipped on a pair of work gloves. We scooped handfuls of wood shavings, scraps of sandpaper, empty cans of wood stain, tubes of foamy spray insulation, and endless cigarette butts. We coughed and wished we had worn surgical masks. After an entire afternoon and several bottles of Sam Adams, we began to see progress. The room, now almost empty, seemed less intimidating than before. We glued sequin eyes on the creepy deer carving and quit, abandoning the barn to watch the sun set from the comfort of our porch.

Construction of flight cages began a few days later. Jesse and I paneled the walls, planned where the doors would go, and discussed what would be best for the birds we'd care for. I staple-gunned plastic sheets to the ceiling while Jesse measured and nailed up a door frame. We imagined a sliding door that could be opened in warm weather, so the birds could fly outside, but closed on cold nights. The sides would have to be made of a mesh small enough to keep bugs in so fledgling insectivores, like orioles and phoebes, could practice hunting. We thought that our plans were perfect, but the longer we worked, the more we began to worry about the structural integrity of the barn itself; the cinderblock foundation seemed to shift slightly after heavy rains, and water pooled in the center of the concrete floor. Would we need drainage? We had some trouble figuring how to attach the door, too, and how to make the outside part of the cage safe from raccoons and other predators—would we need an electric perimeter fence? How would we protect our baby birds?

By fall, the building process had slowed, and by winter, halted altogether. We would wait and see if the barn lasted through the snow and windstorms; if it did, we'd resume building in the spring. In the meantime, Jesse began to use the barn as *his* woodshed. He dragged the sawhorses back inside and separated the usable two-by-fours from the rotten planks. He let his beard grow in. Flannel shirts—missing buttons and covered in fine wood dust—appeared in the laundry hamper. He seemed possessed, and sometimes stayed out in the barn for hours at a time, for entire evenings. Many nights I sat alone on the couch, squinting out into the darkness, listening to the shrieking circular saw and the hoarse rasp of a wood file. The glow from the fluorescent tubes slid out from beneath the elaborate door.

On Christmas, Jesse presented me with a birdhouse made of Carl's lumber, held together by screws and nails from Carl's Mason jars, the edges smoothed by discarded scraps of Carl's sandpaper.

Spring finally began and forced Jesse from the woodshed. He applied to veterinary school and was granted several interviews, taking him away for days at a time. In March, a storm hit while he was away, and the latch on the door between the barn's two rooms broke. From the porch, I could hear the hinges creak when the wind blew through. When the wind grew stronger, the door slammed shut, creaked open, and slammed shut again, like a ghost going in and out, trying to get my attention. When that failed, the wind swept down the ridge and almost ripped the sheets of scalloped metal from the barn's roof.

In April, news of Jesse's acceptances came, and we planned to leave our ridge at the end of the summer. Even though the flight cages were not finished, we took care of injured birds anyway, in parakeet cages and cardboard boxes. We cared for a mallard duckling that had been hit by a car while trying to keep up with his mother. A tire knocked him and sent his downy brown and golden body rolling against the curb. The little duck's inner ear had been damaged so badly by the accident that he couldn't balance himself or eat on his own. To feed him, we had to thread a tube down his throat and push wet cat food and electrolytes in with a syringe. After a week, he gave up and we couldn't save him. I held his delicate, silky body until he cooled and stiffened, while his tiny eyes became dull and chalky. We buried him behind the barn. The world had still been new to him—what a horrible short life he had. By now his bones must be broken toothpicks, dry and dusty.

All the birds we couldn't save we buried behind the barn—a cardinal, a vireo, and a chipping sparrow. But some of the orphans survived, of course. A house finch came to the vet's office, just a few days old, covered only in wispy down and infested with lice. I didn't think he'd make it through the first night, but he did, and for more than two weeks I fed him mushy hand-feeding formula five times a day. Finally, he learned to crack seeds, and I tried to teach him to fly. I'd sit cross-legged in front of the barn and toss him gently; he'd flap his awkward body furiously before falling back to the soft grass. One day, I tossed him and he flew straight up and perched on a branch of a walnut tree, out of my reach. After an hour of chirping at me, perhaps trying to figure out why I wasn't flying up to join him, he swooped back down. He returned for feedings for a few more days before finally taking up with a gang of wild house finches that frequented our bird feeders. He blended with the wild birds and disappeared. Now that I'm gone, I think of him looking for me on the porch, in front of the barn, or in the yard. Is anyone filling the bird feeders I left behind?

We spent the last night in our house wrapping dishes in newspaper and packing them in cardboard boxes. I was wedging a coffee mug between a stack of wrapped dinner plates when I heard a noise outside, a hoarse, breathy growl, like a wood file sheering a plank. The summer breeze knocked pine branches against the window panes. Jesse and I hesitated, and then we went out on the porch with a flashlight. When Jesse panned the light across the trees, the growl rasped again, and he whipped the beam toward it. Clinging to a swaying pine bough were two young screech owls. Their yellow eyes frowned down on us. The smaller of the two still had tufts of fluffy down feathers on the top of his head. Jesse flicked off the light and we crept back inside. Were these owlets the children of our friend with the hole in its wing that we had freed a year earlier? I hoped so. Although the barn was filled with twisted and broken dreams, unfinished projects and discarded plans, someone once planted an orchard here, living proof that some plans pick up on their own where they're dropped. Someone else left peach trees and grapevines. We left screech owls and house finches.

The flight cages were half-finished when we moved away from West Virginia and our home on the ridge. The scraps of our abandoned plans were still scattered in the corners of the barn, our cigarette butts flattened on the concrete floor. I almost hope the wind and the vines finally have their way and strip the barn from the ridge, push its walls onto each other, crumble the cinderblocks and tear the insulation from the support beams, while phantom birds sing from pine boughs above their unmarked graves.

If the barn lasts, will the next occupants of our house clean it out again, and trash all of our unfinished projects? They may never guess we raised orphans inside the barn's sheet metal walls, watched some of them learn to fly and disappear. Maybe the next residents will finish their plans for the ridge. I can imagine their energy and ambition. But sooner than they think, their drive or lives will fade, and they'll leave too, one way or another, their plans half-done, adding their ghosts to the host of dreams swirling like wood dust under the fluorescents.

Laughing Gulls
Peter Makuck

The moon sank in rough seas, a slick
of weak stars, a cold wind from the west,
tall waves tipping into a white seethe.

I'm drawn to this stretch of March sand
where a huge spotlight a half-mile away
is pointed seaward from a motel roof.

Hundreds of gulls flicker like confetti
in the bright beam, cries rip the dark,
white wings plunge into thick schools—

a picture of chaos. But I'm not out here
for solace, just the habit of early
air along this hard unflattering edge.

Every year the tides churn away sand,
swallow boats and swimmers, or send
a bull shark into the shallows for blood.

The wind keens and flattens the sea oats
then suddenly drops to a whisper,
as if to mock my mood, tease me away

from some simple last line. At the motel
when I reach it, the gulls, all of them,
have settled on the surface, a rich lull,

a brilliant spackling of white on black
and a scent of bacon frying that floats out
and sweetens what darkness remains.

Pelicans
DAVID SCOTT

The piper nods at crab holes, ignorant
To anything deeper and a tern plunks
The ocean's hardened surface because he can't
Mine a bigger fish with his light body.
Ax-headed pelicans scour into view
In squads as tight as riot cops or teams
Of combines set to scrape the crop field clean.
With piston-driven wings, they fly the waves
And mow the brake with black ball bearing eyes.
A squall of five bellies scuds the shoreline
Then rises up to glean a glint off scales.
One stalls on air and toughens wings into
The crashing-angle for his accurate drop.
His chest of air and chopping head slice
The ruined water. Clubbed fish, too stunned to flee,
Waits for him to scoop his meal away.
He churns his slapping, ancient feet, regains
The line and its mechanical attack.
Their eyes roll over darkened seas and spark
When deeper flashes break the plane that keeps
The hunt for food from being food. The seasons turn
On days with interlocking teeth. One wing's tip
Opens up the water for an instant.
It closes with a groan toward the shore.

The Handmade Court
Gary Fincke

Building a tennis court was a dream I shared with my father. Constructing it ourselves was his dream alone. But it seemed so easy standing beside him in the middle of June on the land he'd just bought that I estimated the end of July, August tops, the two of us would be spinning out lime along the boundaries, getting things ready for play. He had me captive, because tennis was all I had wanted to do since May when I'd reached the quarterfinals of the biggest junior tournament in Pittsburgh, my rocket-flat serve and forehand good enough for the fourteen-and-unders, even the kids nearly a year older, the ones lucky enough to have birthdays a month or two after the cutoff date of October 1.

The nearest house was a hundred yards away up a dirt road, and my father said there weren't any zoning ordinances that discouraged using your land any way you pleased. "Look at all that clay," he said, and I agreed it looked like we could hold the just-finished French Open right there on our new property if they had postponed it until September. "And this place is nearly level to begin with. We just push this bank over to there, fill in this low spot here, roll it, get some fence, and we're in business."

"All right!" I blurted. I was willing to give up a month of my weekends if it meant using shovels and wheelbarrows and the heavy, water-filled roller that the residents of that nearest house allowed us to store in their garage. This was going to be country club stuff: a clay court, privacy, hours of play without some jerks wearing street shoes telling me and my friends to "get the fuck off the court," meaning any of the only three public courts in Shaler Township in 1959.

A month earlier, my first time in a tournament, I was dressed in plaid swimming trunks and the same white T-shirt I wore under dress shirts on Sunday mornings. Up until that Saturday I'd never worn shorts to play tennis because I didn't own any. I played in old black chinos faded to near-white at the knees, mostly with my father, who wore his green work pants to the pay-by-the-hour county courts ten miles from where we lived.

I had a pair of high-top tennis shoes, and that first Saturday at a tournament I learned that "tennis shoes" was a figurative expression. I wasn't allowed on the clay courts where the youngest entries were being shuttled, so I had to wait (and so did my angry opponent) for a default to occur on one of the hard courts so that we could play. Tennis shoes, I was told by the tournament director, had flat soles. They were low-cut and lighter, and they weren't black like my Keds.

I had two tennis rackets at least, the ones my father and mother used. They were right off the discount store counter, pre-strung with string so cheap it shredded into what looked like unraveling cardboard. No one else in the tournament wore shorts that weren't white.

Fourth of July weekend, a couple of days before my fourteenth birthday, I found myself starting the first work I'd ever done that amounted to anything other than earning an extra dessert. As soon as I filled one wheelbarrow and hauled the clay to be dumped, I was sweating. In half an hour I had blisters, and there was no sign of an ice cream break.

Because my father's new property was nearly an hour's drive each way from our house, once there he was committed to a full day of work. This early in the project, whining was out of the question. The only antidote to pain was planning lines I could use on girls when the muscles that would surely come from the hardest work I'd ever done bulged and rippled beside every swimming pool I could get myself invited to.

Where I played tennis with my friends, there were nets with holes so large they resembled the webs torn by the struggles of victims captured by giant spiders in the movies I watched on late-night television. Men in blue jeans who used the same skinhead balls all summer would lean on those nets to swill beer after thirty minutes of loping around barechested. By the end of May, even if the park service repaired the worst holes in April before they put the nets back up after a winter in some storage garage, the net strings would tear away from the tape that ran across the top so you might, every once in a while, skid a shot through a hole without fluttering a bit of cord. If your opponent wasn't paying attention, the point continued.

For placing legitimate shots, however, cross-court was best. Although there were times we found the net pulled straight across by men who thought it needed to be the same level from side to side, it always sagged, when we lowered it, into a sad, shallow U because there was no center strap to adjust for tension.

The second day of that tournament, I added a cardigan sweater that was a cheap knockoff of what Perry Como wore on television every Saturday. It had red and blue cuffs and a similar stripe where it buttoned up the front. I'd noticed that the better players had v-neck sweaters; they had racket covers and strings that were gold or clear. And their rackets said Wilson and Bancroft rather than Best Craft like mine, the least of my worries, because when I laid my mother's racket on the ground by the net post, it wobbled slightly from being warped. Worse, one of the strings was broken and tied off—my father saved a few dollars, waiting until at least three strings broke before he took the rackets to the Honus Wagner store in Pittsburgh where they were replaced with those same woven-nylon shredders.

The second time my opponent served he looped a short, underhanded shot into the service box that I caught on the second hop. I thought he'd lost track of the score and was slapping the ball my way until he moved to the other side of the court to serve. Five minutes later, standing six feet behind the baseline, I caught a ball still in the air like I always did so I wouldn't have to chase it. "My point," my opponent said, and he walked so casually to receive my next serve that I was sure he was right.

"Don't be discouraged, son. He's seeded four," the man who collected the used balls said from outside the fence. I didn't say anything. I didn't know what "seeded" meant. Ten minutes later, when that boy sprained his ankle, I took my default win and moved on. My mother, when I got home, presented me with a pair of white tennis shorts and a shirt with a collar to wear the following day.

I won that match, too, defeating a boy who was seeded number eight. He threw his racket over the fence seven times during the match. His mother retrieved it each time. When we finished, he dragged his v-neck sweater by one sleeve, sweeping a path from the net post to the gate.

That first afternoon of building, I'd been digging for almost two hours when I nearly speared myself as my shovel struck rock. "Dammit," I said, and my father spun around with his shovel loaded. I ducked, thinking I was eating a face-full for swearing. "Sorry, Dad," I said, when the dirt stayed put.

"What's the problem?" my father asked, so tolerant that I turned nervous.

"It's like there's a road under here, a big rock or something."

"Work around it. Find the edge and pry it out. Nobody said there wouldn't be any rocks. You can't expect everything to be simple."

My father often spoke like that, short answers broken up by phrases I didn't realize were platitudes. What did I know, just out of confirmation class at church and still an acolyte? I was donning a surplice once a month so I could light and snuff candles beside an altar. There was hope, though, because I'd just been invited by Janet Cook to a semiformal dance at the club her parents belonged to.

I poked around with the shovel blade, and when I'd measured the perimeter of the rock, I understood that we were not going to finish this court in time to help my chances in the fourteens. "Dad," I said, "it's four feet across; it's twice that around."

My father stood staring at me, performing a quick mental assessment of the personification of his genes. He didn't look like he was enjoying the evaluation. "You work over here, if that's what you want," he finally said. "No boulders over here. No mountains."

"Really," I said, "there's no moving this thing."

"There's always moving. It doesn't go down forever like a hole to China."

"You'll see."

"Over here, then. Over here so you can at least be shoveling while I get the Himalayas out of your way."

I didn't back off very far. This was an opportunity to rest for a minute. My father was about to recognize that this project was a disaster. He'd cancel the remainder of the work order before he'd remember to complain about me standing around.

"Looks as if you're going to learn what real work is," my father observed after he'd probed long enough to make it look like he'd done the measuring. "Get the pick from the garage."

I was in the quarterfinals. This boy was seeded number three, and by now the strings on my father's racket were frayed so badly it looked, from a distance, as if there were a hole in the middle. During the last game of the first set, three strings broke during one point, my last forehand slingshotting over my opponent's head as if I'd imagined him Goliath. I picked up my mother's racket, my ready-made excuse for losing in the one-sided fashion you might expect if you used a lightweight racket that was warped and missing a string.

The truth is I would have lost even with a Wilson Jack Kramer Autograph Model in my hand. I had a fast, flat first serve and a forehand I hit harder than any boy my age. But I ran around every shot to avoid my backhand, and then ran back to a makeshift middle I created five feet to the left of center. It was easier to sprint to wide forehands than to run around backhands, and my opponent had made certain I was doing both on every point.

The other boy's father, sympathetic perhaps, took me aside to explain that I was using what was called a playground grip, the same grip my father used. I could only slice a backhand. If I tried to hit a backhand hard, the ball traveled directly into the bottom of the net. "You get yourself some lessons," the man said. "Learn how to play the game."

It was the same summer my uncle took me aside after church and said it was time I stopped tying my tie in a "nigger knot" like my father did if I were going to a semiformal dance at the private tennis and swimming pool club where Janet Cook's parents and their friends had two well-kept courts for themselves. He stood me in front of a mirror in the men's room and had me master the Full Windsor. "There," he said, and he left the rest to my memory without saying a word about the origin of the name of the knot I vowed never to tie again.

I walked into that dance with confidence in my tie, but I didn't need my uncle to explain to me that I was badly dressed when none of the boys were wearing a sport coat like the one I'd gotten that week. "Just like new," my father had said, but my cousin had worn it for the past two years, and before that his older brother had worn it for three more.

It didn't matter that it was a good fit. The difference between being new in 1954 and 1959, from lapel width to pattern design, was clear.

Walking away from my struggling father, I maintained a steady cadence up the lane toward the garage by telling myself it was worth it having to split stone like I was on a chain gang just so I didn't have to hear again how stupid I was for claiming the rock unmovable. Nevertheless, I took as long as possible finding the pick. I wasn't in a hurry to swing anything that had the feel of the John Henry legend about it.

I lugged the pick back down the lane. The head of it looked to me like it had been forged in the nineteenth century and dragged across Pennsylvania while its owner had to scour the countryside for Indians. Though it was the only pick I'd ever handled, I was suddenly sure my father owned something from the Iron Age. I carted it across the clay to the monstrous rock, and before my father could start instructing, took what I thought was the correct stance, swinging the ancient tool up over my head the way I'd seen it being done in all those *Boys' Life* features on diligence and fortitude.

The heavy head slid down the shaft and split open two of my fingers. "Dammit, shit!" I yelled.

"Being ignorant doesn't mean you have to be stupid," my father said. "You ought to count yourself lucky you had one hand up so high, or you'd need more than swearing to cure you. You break your hand and there's no point in us finishing this thing here."

"I'm hopeless," I said. "I'm too dumb to live."

"Sarcasm doesn't help anybody."

"I need leg irons. I need a striped suit and one of those beanies."

"You go for a walk," he said. "You get your head clear while I take care of this." And I did, walking to where the people who lived in the nearest house were watching television on their porch. As soon as I paused to look over their shoulders, they invited me to sit down. The Pirates were on. I watched five innings while my father swung that pick against rock.

My next tournament, in early July, was entirely on clay courts, but by then I had real tennis shoes. Like the big tournament in May, it was held in an area of Pittsburgh where the streets were shaded and the yards were professionally landscaped. The mothers who sat along the fences were dressed in stylish skirts and blouses, and all of them wore sunglasses. The fathers who watched all wore dress shirts and ties, their suit coats left on hangers that were hooked to the inside of their cars.

By now I had a knit shirt with a collar to wear and a Bancroft tennis racket (with lousy spiral-nylon strings because my mother had bought it pre-strung). My father, foregoing sleep before his night shift in the bakery he owned, stood throughout the two matches I played before I lost in the round of sixteen to an unseeded player, double-faulting fifteen times because I was trying to serve with the proper grip. Both days he wore a white T-shirt and his dark green work pants. Those courts were so perfect that when I saw a few small green leaves pushing up through the clay at the base of the fence, I bent down and uprooted them.

The next weekend my father and I worked on the court, we discovered another stone stretched out like the continental shelf. I decided to give logic a try: "I say we give this up," I repeated three times, hoping that the tumblers in my father's brain would fall. I saw that the summer was going to disappear while we slaved in this rock garden. The weekend's late afternoons, when I should be perfecting the shots that would bring me trophies, were going to repeat themselves as times for physical exhaustion.

"We did one giant, we can do two," my father added, using an inaccurate personal pronoun.

I didn't see the proof for his syllogism. "The first one's still in the way," I pointed out.

"It's almost done," he said. "It's a day's work now."

I estimated how many times we'd have to split the newest discovery in order to size the pieces for carrying. "You keep at it with the shovel," my father ordered. "I'll work the pick. An extra weekend or two is all. You'll see."

My mother was the one who drove me to the next tournament because their starting times were in the morning and early afternoons on weekdays. Even at ten a.m., though, there were fathers in ties at the courts. What did they do, I wondered, that let them sit charting shots at every tournament?

My mother had sunglasses at least. She brought a folding lawn chair because, she explained, she knew how long these matches could take. But after one round I drew the number one seed, and even with half as many double faults as I'd had in the previous tournament, I won three games altogether. "He's a year older," my mother consoled me. "He'll have to play with the older boys next year."

I shook my head. There was only one more tournament before school started, and it was played at a country club my mother had described as "snooty."

It didn't matter. I lost in the first round to the best player in the twelve-and-unders, a skinny boy who was playing the fourteens, his mother told mine, "for the experience."

By the third week of August the tennis court project was a shamble of rock strewn from seventeen boulders we'd found. On the next-to-last summer weekend, I stood among them, not one trophy in hand for my year in the fourteens, and I was thinking about how useless my work had been, how flat and unstable my ground strokes still were, how every court but the ones I practiced on had nets that rose, as they should, six inches higher on each side. The stunted beginning of a stone wall ran along one side of the court. "It will get high enough we won't even need fence on that side," my father explained. "People can sit on it while they're waiting to play. Your friends, if they have a mind to come out this far for a day of tennis."

"Nobody wants to sit on a bunch of stones, Dad," I said.

"They do it all the time. In parks. On hikes."

"In old clothes they don't care about."

"You play tennis in a suit?"

"White shorts, Dad. Think about it."

"I'll sit on it then. Your friends from the swim club can stand. They can make sure they don't sweat, too."

My mother, after I told her I wouldn't go anywhere ever again in my lousy hand-me-down sport coat, said, "Only if it doesn't fit."

Because our church wasn't air-conditioned and there hadn't been another dance, I hadn't worn the coat in over a month. I put it on and concentrated on the sleeves, extending my arms to give them every chance of being too long.

"They're okay," she said, but she tugged the fat lapels together and frowned. "It's tight in the chest," she said. "You'll look silly in this before you know it."

I inhaled before she could let go of the material. "Okay," she said, "but don't tell your father. It'll be our little secret until the weather turns cooler. All that digging in the dirt must be doing you some good."

Over Labor Day weekend I watched my father loop a chain around one of the thirty leftover fragments from the biggest stones we'd found, a mid-size one that was going to be a test. I followed his face while he worked, noticing how his jaw jerked, how his lips and teeth told secrets about self-absorption. Each time my father yanked at the chain, the stone heaved and slid a few inches. It could have been the cornerstone for a pyramid. "See," he said. "Just a little bending of the back is all it takes. Just some elbow grease."

It took my father five minutes to stop and start his way thirty feet to where the stones stretched along the lane. I watched him walk backwards and tug, walk forwards and pull, horselike, and I grew certain that I wouldn't be able to shift one of those stones more than the length of my body, that my father was going to be forced to remove every one of them unless he expected me to kneel and push each boulder from behind while he was dragging it with the chain.

During my first week in ninth-grade geography we studied farming practices, how different cultures worked to prevent erosion, and as I looked at the pictures of ruined crop lands, I could see how the tennis court was going to wash away with each rain because water poured over the bank we'd cut and the knobbed end of another huge stone we'd exposed, a delta of small channels branching into where a service court would be. I knew I needed a backhand, too, and a second serve that had enough spin so I could accomplish something besides pushing it into play next year and having kids who understood plane geometry smash it back past me for winners.

"See?" my father said the next weekend, pointing to how only a half-dozen stones were left on the court surface. "You see how things get done?"

"Sure," I agreed.

"And see how high that wall's gotten? A fence would be a waste there."

"I don't know, Dad."

"How many balls you miss-hit high off to the side like that? Two, three a match?"

"Something like that. Maybe more. It depends."

"You're fourteen already. Maybe next year you won't miss-hit more than one or two balls a match. Maybe none."

There were networks of furrows from the dragged stones. My father saw me looking at them. "You get to them with the roller and it's good as new."

"Yeah."

"We're playing here in two weeks. We don't have to wait until everything's perfect for that. It's not a country club we're building here."

I calculated how much of an advantage it would be to serve toward the end where the water was eating at where the service court would be. My father jerked at the chain he'd wrapped around one of the last boulders. Somewhere in one of the trees across the lane there were squirrels I couldn't see scrabbling along branches, but my father was straining so close next to me that I started to count his steps. He stopped and started twenty-three times before he worried the rock to the wall, never taking more than three choppy steps on any lunge.

Crows in the Morning, Crows in the Evening
CHRISTIEN GHOLSON

Sunset snowclouds white-out Niowat Ridge:
What was sunlipped is now forgot, gone down
a crystal hallway of snow-mirror drifts snaking over
black shine of reservoir ice, braids of snow dust
shocked up and over the concrete dam,
sails body-flung spread crazy as the crow's fight with the wind,
wing over wing, turbine spun black
banking in veils above the ghost-tin of an ice creek bed,
thin as moonlight, thin as a voice made of snow
melting against the dome of a broke streetlight

      someone says "begin"
                    but we can't tell where the voice is coming from

The shed door's loose, bangs against the shed wall,
snow across the roof, so many blankets, chiasmus
of bluelight loops from the top of my skull
down my spine, between my legs, yours, up
through the middle of your body, your hair,
arcs into the zenith of my head, like the prism in a lone cloud
I saw above a pine ridge on the bus yesterday,
a shattered sun spread smooth as the marine inside
of an abalone shell, same as the inside of the mind
when it's turned inside out, exposed to light and outside
it's desire in the shape of a leaf frozen in ice,
broken off from the sing-edge of a creek bank,
water-moil black beneath the covers,
slow melt sheets over thumbstone, suncracked grain
rockjut and jutrock over and under juniper twist calligraphy

Christien Gholson

      someone says "middle"
           still can't tell where the voice is coming from—the roof?

Snow grains skid over tarpaper
the way a crow says nothing when it barks three times into the wind
sitting on the streetlight pole out the front door, no beginning,
no meaning under candle shadow, wrapped in nothing but crows,
crows in the morning, crows in the evening,
the sentinel crow leftover from some lost Donner party
stands in the kitchen sink before dawn, stares
at the faucet, waits for the moon's reflection in a sudden drop,
black eye reflecting the glass surface of the moon's sea, my cheek
across your smooth belly when the dirt streets still have no snow tracks,
no moonrabbits to bare their perfect snow-teeth

      someone says "end"
           but our ears are attached to our fingers
             and it passes over us unheard

The water from the broken toilet is the slip-sheet falling,
water spilling under ice laced into itself, ledge pool following pool,
and you know you're not done with crows, there's going to be one
on the toilet tank in the bathroom come storm-morning after,
he won't mention the weather but get straight to the point, say:
"Do you remember what you saw this morning when you woke?"
A profoundly moral question he thinks
not knowing each of your fingers has a name, a name
the same way the stones are stacked in the barrier wall
next to the shed, a name
the same way leather boots by the sliding glass door
fill with moonlight while outside the glass are black wells
where the boots made print shadows in the snow, a name
the way tire tread on the road's shoulder holds the silhouette of a
                                        ponderosa,
the way the branch overhang has the same high-pitched sing and drift
of snow dust over a snow curve by the shed, the shed door
banging against the shed walls again, a name the same as
blackweed pokes through snow

bending, straightening

    each finger to my mouth a name
    the way the stones are stacked
    each finger across my back a name
    the way the stones are stacked

that awkward angle of each stone
                        the dark space between

The Edge Effect
Sarah Gorham

You may have noticed. Spreading your towel over a thin strip of sand below the dunes and near the Atlantic, what usually matters is the angle of sun. But just this once, you observe the beach is dense with animal and vegetable action. Is it the time of day? The lack of humidity? Maybe.

More likely, this abundant activity has to do with *where* you've planted your picnic basket. It's called the "edge effect," an ecological term to describe what happens when two contrasting biomes—forest and field, ocean and shore, and most recently, wild and developed or disturbed land—blend, a territory called the ecotone.

This overlap, this edge effect, produces double the ordinary plant life, nesting, predation, and most importantly, the rampant growth of opportunistic species. Poison ivy is one example. We're all familiar with that weed, one of the first to populate an ecotone. Here's another one: the sea rocket, common along the edges of dune and water. This extraordinary member of the *Cruciferae* family has the most amazing seedpods: like small two-stage rockets, they pop apart easily. Both sections are filled with seeds: one section has a corky substance that allows it to float away during high tide and populate new areas; the other remains with the mother plant, buries itself in the sand, and eventually produces a new plant. Thus, the sea rocket both stays its ground and easily expands into new territory. Ingenious.

Modern development in wilderness areas—new housing tracts, highways, malls—has led increasingly to areas of mixed biomes or ecotones. The very same thing is happening in creative writing. Literature is today, quite clearly, in a period of overlap and integration. Just as in the natural world, we have seen certain species of *literature* benefit opportunistically, and, in fact, *new species develop* as a result of the edge effect, of living along the borders between poetry and prose. We have poems that look like prose, stories that resemble poems, and essays that abandon most of the requirements of the form in favor of poetic techniques. In fact, as Christine Hume pointed out in a recent review in the online journal *Constant Critic*, two new poetry presses—Slope Editions and Verse Press (which is now an imprint of Wave Books in Seattle)—both began their publishing ventures with books of prose: Joe Wenderoth's novel, *Letters to Wendy*, and Jenny Boully's *The Body*, an essay in the form of footnotes.

The three most prominent of these edge species are the prose poem, the short short, and the lyric essay. But every so-called "innovation" usually has some precursor in the distant or not-so-distant past. Blended genres are no exception.

For example, paper was very costly in the Middle Ages. Because of this, a certain economy of white space developed: verse was transcribed without lineation, sometimes even without spacing, in order to save parchment—written by necessity, as it were, in prose. Texts were written in two versions, verse and prose, for two different audiences, learned and lay. Writers of metrical texts might also place a prose paraphrasal in a facing column.

As anyone who has read Shakespeare knows, characters in plays often shift between verse and prose to signal weightier thoughts or crashing emotion. Changes in genre are also used by a playwright to differentiate characters or the social rank of characters—the paradigm case is Shakespeare's *Midsummer Night's Dream*, where the nobles speak blank verse, the fairies couplets, and the minor characters (soldiers, guards, etc.) prose.

In fiction, there's Nabokov's *Pale Fire*, Pushkin's *Eugene Onegin* and, more recently, Vikram Seth's *The Golden Gate*, all novels set in verse. Expository texts were often cast in verse to aid memorization, including works on law, medicine, philosophy, math, grammar, botany, zoology, astronomy, physics, history, and genealogy.

For various reasons financial, sociological, psychological, educational, and aesthetic, there has been, for a long time, much mingling between our two biomes, poetry and prose.

We can most likely agree that there are some basic qualities to the poetry side of the ecotone: Stephen Minot's definition is among the best, and describes five fundamentals: 1) the line as primary unit rather than the sentence; 2) imagery, a heightened use of simile, metaphor, and symbol; 3) sound; 4) rhythm; and 5) density, implying far more than is stated directly. To this I would add the use of "gaps," or associative leaps.

And the prose side of the ecotone? 1) Use of the sentence instead of the line as punctuation provides the breathing space and the rhythms; 2) in fiction, character, plot, setting, and theme; and 3) in creative nonfiction, a basic engagement with facts and personal experience. For the sake of simplicity, I'll ignore journalism and the scholarly or formal essay, in which art takes a backseat to the conveyance of information.

1. The Prose Poem

The first edge species, the prose poem, has now become very familiar. Peter Johnson, its tireless champion, said this by way of definition: "Just as black humor straddles the fine line between comedy and tragedy, so the prose poem plants one foot in prose, the other in poetry, both heels resting precariously on banana peels."

Prose poems take from poetry: fragmentation, compression, repetition, rhyme, density of emotion, depth—unity, even in brevity. From prose, they borrow the sentence and the paragraph that function as stanzas. The word stanza derives from the Italian for "room." The room that a prose poem occupies is as far as the margins will allow, and it seeks to utilize that space with language, not furniture.

The prose poem is very flexible—suitable for ambivalence, fable, surrealism, and narrative. It was first advanced by Aloysius Bertrand in his book *Gaspard de la Nuit*, published in 1842 and widely recognized as the pioneering work of prose-poetry. Following Bertrand's lead, Baudelaire snatched up the form and called it "petites poèmes en prose." With the exception of Gertrude Stein, the American modernists Eliot, Pound, and Stevens didn't really take up the form with any enthusiasm. In the seventies, the prose poem reappeared with Russell Edson, Jorge Luis Borges, and Robert Bly, but it was still seen as the black sheep, an odd duck, a genre that no one knew what to do with. It's only recently that prose poems have become truly fashionable, and they *are* fashionable now.

Here's an example, by Robert Hass, from his collection *Human Wishes*:

The Story of the Body

The young composer, working that summer at an artist's colony, had watched her for a week. She was Japanese, a painter, almost sixty, and he thought he was in love with her. He loved her work, and her work was like the way she moved her body, used her hands, looked at him directly when she made amused and considered answers to his questions. One night, walking back from a concert, they came to her door and she turned to him and said, "I think you would like to have me. I would like that too, but I must tell you that I have had a double mastectomy," and when he didn't understand, "I've lost both my breasts." The radiance that he had carried around in his belly and chest cavity—like music—withered very quickly, and he made himself look at her when he said, "I'm sorry. I don't think I could." He walked back to his own cabin through the pines, and in the morning he found a small blue bowl on the porch outside his door. It looked to be full of rose petals, but he found when he picked it up that the rose petals were on top; the rest of the bowl—she must have swept them from the corners of her studio—was full of dead bees.

What a stark and moving image this poem ends with: the rose petals atop a bowl of dead bees. Both symbols of fertility and propagation, of course, but twisted slightly to reflect the man's harsh rejection of the woman's body. Is this gift then retaliation for the man's selfishness, or an act of forgiveness? It's not clear. And what a poet Hass is, ending with an image, leaving the question unanswered. The options are not explicated; the poem finishes with "an emotional/intellectual complex in a moment of time," as Pound described.

Hass has some interesting things to say about prose poems. He began writing them in the seventies when the form was used as "a kind of wacky surrealist work," as if avoiding as much as possible the conventions of expository or narrative prose. Surrealism, at least, was undeniably poetic. "So almost as soon as I started working," he said in an interview, "I got interested in those boundaries: what the prose poem *wasn't* supposed to sound like . . . Later, I was working in these forms because they had a certain outwardness that verse didn't have. Things were going on in my life that I didn't want to look at, didn't want to feel. And I wanted to keep writing, so I unconsciously started writing prose to avoid the stricter demands of incantation. When I was doing it, it seemed to be exploratory; in retrospect, it seems a sort of long escape...."

To Hass, the confines of poetic form forced intimacy with those things in his life he didn't want to face, and prose offered him an escape, perhaps because he was dipping someone else's narratives into the story? Conversely, the late Robert Creeley was once asked why his poems in *For Love* were so formal, written in relatively tight, metrically measured stanzas. He responded by saying that during his twenties and early thirties, his emotional life was chaotic; he needed the form to organize his feelings.

2. The Short Short

The basic elements of fiction are plot, character, setting, and theme. By this token, Hass's poem is a story. There are two characters, a plot, a setting, and least two themes—forgiveness and retribution, as well as the sexual life of a diseased body.

But Hass's piece also borrows from poetry a heightened perception, experience, and consciousness. Though it eschews lines, stanzas, and regular meter, its language is nevertheless highly musical. We know we are in the hands of a poet with the startling use of image, the comparison of the Japanese woman's artwork to her body's movement, the description of the radiance, the music dying in the composer's belly. If this were a short short, we would have to say the story is highly lyrical, influenced deeply by poetry. Ah, the distinctions blur already.

The issue is further complicated in another prose paragraph by Lydia Davis, published in *Samuel Johnson Is Indignant*, a collection of stories:

Happiest Moment

If you ask her what is a favorite story she has written, she will hesitate for a long time and then say it may be this story that she read in a book once: an English language teacher in China asked his Chinese student to say what was the happiest moment in his life. The student hesitated for a long time. At last he smiled with embarrassment and said that his wife had once gone to Beijing and eaten duck there, and she often told him about it, and he would have to say the happiest moment in his life was her trip, and the eating of the duck.

In this brief piece Davis has created a perfect example of a postmodern short short. To use postmodern terms, there are in fact four discourse communities or pockets of meaning within this little story: the "you" asking "her" what her favorite story is, the writer with her book, the English language teacher in China with his Chinese student, and the student with his wife who traveled in Beijing. We are very far removed from the moment of happiness promised in the title.

But that is the point. As the theory goes, we are in an age of alienation and distance from the genuine experience or object or emotional truth. Because of mass production, mass information, and the media, we are dealing only with copies—copies of copies of copies, simulacra, like the head repeated endlessly in a barbershop mirror. Even within Davis's four discourse communities, there is removal and distance. The writer answers the question incorrectly—not a story she has written, but one she has read. The Chinese student answers his question not with his direct instance of happiness, but with his *wife's* experience of eating duck. In Hungarian literary critic George Lukács's terms, "The concrete universal is replaced by an abstract particularity." All the specifics of this short short, even the delicious duck, are "abstract particularities," at least one step back from the thing itself. And the "concrete universal," *happiness*—anchored in one specific moment of consuming duck in Bejing—is seriously thwarted.

In her article "Flashes on the Meridian: Dazzled by Flash Fiction" Pamelyn Casto lists the various nicknames for this hybrid we are calling short shorts: flash fiction, of course, but also sudden-, postcard-, minute-, furious-, fast-, quick-, skinny-, and micro-fiction. The French call their short shorts *nouvelles*. In China this type of writing has several interesting names: little short story, pocket-size story, minute-long story, and the smoke-long story (just long enough to read while smoking a cigarette).

From poetry, short shorts borrow density and spareness. From prose, the sentence and narrative push—though as we have seen these are elements available to poetry too.

The short short can be as brief as three words ("Richard Corey died.") or as long as 1,500. It generally falls between one hundred and 750. And, briefly, it tells a story. Due to its size, it is sometimes extremely condensed, often forceful with abrupt beginnings and endings.

Like poetry, it insinuates, rather than explicates. By necessity, it employs white space in place of exposition, background, descriptions of setting, and character appearance. A character may be drawn with a few spoken words. The short short allows us to travel from point A to point B without laying out every brick.

Some of the very best short shorts are those of Yasunari Kawabata, the Nobel Laureate. Kawabata is best known for what he calls "palm-of-the-hand" stories, the earliest published in 1920 and the last appearing in 1972, posthumously. J. Martin Holman's *The Dancing Girl of Izu and Other Stories* collected translations of the tales, including twenty that had been published originally in Japanese before 1930. They are quintessentially Japanese in their resemblance to Zen painting or haiku, relying on suggestion and intimation, rather than exposition and statement. This is what Kenneth Koch says about them in his review: "They make writing a story seem—and it may be—as natural a result of deep excited feeling as *writing a poem.*"

3. The Lyric Essay

The lyric essay is another recent hybrid, the sea rocket of our literary world, a wonderful species that lives balanced precariously between poetry and essay. The term was coined by John D'Agata, though he refuses to claim ownership. He serves as essay editor of the *Seneca Review*, and a few years ago, edited an all-lyric essay issue of the magazine. Since then, he has published a terrific anthology called *The Next American Essay*, published by Graywolf Press, which anyone interested in the genre should read.

In this anthology is an essay in the form of footnotes, an essay composed of bumper stickers, essays constructed by strung-together aphorisms, an essay titled "The Marionette Theater" that once appeared in a book of theater criticism, but that really tells you very little about marionettes, a list of "Things to Do," as well as more conventional essays by John McPhee, Joan Didion, and Annie Dillard. The book is structured deliberately, beginning with these icons, then sashaying into the brave new world of authors such as Susan Griffin, Thalia Field, and Joe Wenderoth.

D'Agata has also published his own collection of lyric essays, *Halls of Fame*, also from Graywolf. Appropriately, he has two MFAs from Iowa: one in poetry and one in creative nonfiction. In several interviews and articles online, he has offered an articulate, explorative definition of the lyric essay: From poetry, the lyric essay takes density, distillation of ideas, musicality, and associative leaps. From the essay it borrows the use of sentence, instead of line.

Most traditional essays present an argument. The lyric essay may obstruct that argument, or, as in some poetry, refuse to come to a conclusion, or present confusion instead. At its extreme, it may be without story, theme, or climax. Not content to merely explain or confess, it may be an attempt at making sense of something. And with this, D'Agata harkens back to the French definition of the word essay or *essayer*, to try.

From its traditional roots, the lyric essay takes a basic desire to engage with facts. However, the lyric essay charges those facts with imagination. Lyric essayists organize reality, fill in the blank spaces, or omit unnecessary, uninteresting details. As Emerson said, "There are no facts, only art."

For poets, this slant truth, this sketchy engagement with reality, is nothing new. It's called "poetic license." As Charles Simic says, "Poetry is one activity in life where consummate liars are not only admired but completely trusted. Of course, the hope for any poem is that it will convince the reader that this is exactly what happened, even if it did not.... The relationship between reality and imagination keeps changing from poet to poet, and even from poem to poem, so that often seems to be one turns out to be the other, or more confusingly, a mixture of the two."

Try as we might to present facts without commentary or elaboration or interpretation, the lyric essay and poetry share a simple truth—the mere presence of an observer, the mere act of telling, means necessarily that we will be distorting or enhancing those facts in some way. Our bodies are situated between two biomes: fact and imagination. Another edge effect is this electric, potent, and yes, blurred area between the two.

Here's an example of a short lyric essay, which author Ann Carson calls a talk:

On Reading

Some fathers hate to read but love to take the family on trips. Some children hate trips but love to read. Funny how often these find themselves passengers in the same automobile. I glimpsed the stupendous clear-cut boulders of the Rockies from between paragraphs of *Madame*

Bovary. Cloud shadows roved languidly across her huge rock throat, traced her fir flanks. Since those days, I do not look at hair on female flesh without thinking, Deciduous?

Carson establishes the argument at once. Two characters (though they are presented as "some" fathers and "some" children) have opposing interests, traveling and reading, respectively. They are crammed together in a car, zooming through the Rockies. Carson then offers two illustrations of what happens when you overlap these concerns: Boulders drop into the pages of *Madame Bovary*; the Frenchwoman herself appears in the mountains among the clouds with a huge rock throat and fir flanks. These surreal images accurately grasp the experience of intense reading. As Carson concludes, the world that reading reveals is a very strange and indelible mixture of physical reality and imagination. And it changes our vision forever.

What I love most about this piece is the jump she makes from her introductory statements. She doesn't lay out the plodding pathway. She just goes there, assuming the reader will follow. And we do.

Helen Vendler says of the lyric poem, "It depends on gaps . . . . It is suggestive rather than exhaustive." Rosemarie Waldrop calls this attention to the white spaces between text "gap gardening." She adds: "When the smooth horizontal travel of eye/mind is impeded, when the connection is broken, there is a kind of orchestral meaning that comes about in the break, a vertical dimension made up of the energy field between the two lines (or phrases or sentences). A meaning that both connects and illuminates the gap, so that the shadow zone of silence between the elements gains weight, become an element of the structure."

The lyric essay uses gaps, too. As in poems, the reader is invited to make her own connections between blocks of text. The overall argument of the essay, if there is one, may meander, digress, come at the subject from a huge variety of angles. Just as the reader may throw up her arms in exasperation, wondering, *what is the point?* the essay may finally narrow and land on its target. Or a series of seemingly unrelated paragraphs or fragments will gain meaning by juxtaposition alone.

"The essay acts as if all subjects are linked to each other," D'Agata notes. Maybe you've had this experience before: When in the midst of writing a poem, in your total absorption, you look up and notice that the world has changed—everything you see somehow relates. Your mind has become a huge magnet: rather than having to rummage around for interesting details, facts come to *you*. While writing this essay, I spotted a pregnant woman and thought: women in general are more comfortable with edge effects. Their bodies are in a constant state of flux, fertile nesting grounds, territories that mix past and future. Indeed the child itself is an opportunistic species, a blend of father and mother. A storm system was moving in that day, a cold front overlapping a warm front, with an edge effect of dangerous, turbulent weather. I saw a drawing on the cover of the *New York Times's* "Week in Review" section: red-circle Republicans overlapping blue-circle Democrats, and the muddy marquise in between for those hapless citizens who do not precisely fit, but carry allegiances to both parties or "biomes."

There are extreme examples of the use of collage and of gaps. A surrealist parlor game starts with half the players writing "if" statements and the other half "then" statements, after which the moderator shuffles the writings together as one haphazard work of art. In a manuscript I saw recently, the author collected about thirty openings of essay, story, anecdote, and scholarly treatise, juxtaposing them with conclusions from various essays, stories, anecdotes and scholarly treatises. They were spliced together randomly, at least it so appeared, so that the reader found herself straining to find the connections. The individual pieces were funny, beautifully written, and often brilliant, but the gaps were enormous.

Whether or not you like this kind of gap in prose or poetry depends upon your comfort in such a place. Questions arise: Is it laziness or courage on the writer's part not to draw the pieces together into some semblance of meaning? Is it laziness on the reader's part not to want to do the work it takes to create the meaning, the connections between texts? Is it absolutely necessary to make meaning at all? Can we live with that? I believe the world is not a chaotic place, as some of the more radical use of collage seems to imply; I think we'll discover more order, more connective tissue, not less, as time goes by. My philosophic and aesthetic allegiance therefore leans towards Hass and Carson, who employ more traditional uses of gaps in their prose poems and essays.

At the same time, I'm excited by the more radical forays into the ecotone, and feel it is important for both prose writers and poets to have tolerance for experimentation, which isn't always successful, and sometimes looks silly or clumsy or at the very least, rough, in its effort to move literature forward. D'Agata himself is well aware the lyric essay is not quite there yet. Indeed, as several people have noted, the *Next American Essay* anthology ends with a list essay called "Things to Do," by Joe Wenderoth.

Here's a ten-second essay by James Richardson, from his collection *Vectors: Aphorisms and Ten Second Essays*.

407.

When I re-married, I started remembering things—the smell of yarrow, words of my father—I hadn't thought of in years, as if they had suddenly become necessary to the new self that was organizing. The mind is like a well-endowed museum, only a small fraction of its holdings on view at any one time, and this is true from hour to hour as well as from era to era. I am different tones, capacities, intelligences, memories when I am phoning on business, walking by the canal, or waiting with that finely tensed blankness for a line to write itself. For the most part, there is nothing romantic about the unconscious. It starts as the sentences we did not say, the love we did not use. It is as substantial or insubstantial as the shadow of a house, in which some things will grow, some not. Which moves as the sun moves.

This is a beautifully balanced lyric essay. It borrows a great deal from the personal essay, in that it is intimate, trusting right from the start that the reader has something in common with the speaker. It travels towards deeper levels of thought and wisdom. It moves like the mind moves, back and forth between physical detail and direct statement, between inside, hermetic experience and outside, public revelation. It even mimics the traditional five-paragraph essay, with its first sentence the thesis, elaboration upon that theme being the second, evidence as example in the third sentence, the turn or the spin at the fourth sentence, and the haunting image to conclude the essay.

But this essay also works like a poem. How often have we, like the speaker in this essay, begun our poems with description, a tallying of what we see or hear or smell. Gradually, if we are writing well, this leads to the insight—in this case, the mind like a well-endowed museum. Then Richardson leaps further (there's that gap): our various actions call up various holdings in this museum. Whether we are walking, waiting, or writing, our subconscious supplies the shading, the tones, intelligences, memories. Richardson then contradicts what he began with in the poem: this sudden recall, this access to the subconscious, is not exclusively a result of romance: it is the result of *any* action or experience. Or it isn't. The subconscious is not only like a shadow, it is like a *moving* shadow. Because we, like the sun, are always moving. The essay, like a poem, is extraordinarily compressed and satisfying in its surprising flips in direction, its "moves," its layers and layers of substance, dense and active, just what I like to see coming out of the ecotone.

All of these examples use the paragraph as basic structure. I chose them deliberately, as I was interested in illustrating the ripe confusion along the edges of genre, the literary ecotone. What are we dealing with? Poetry? Story? Essay? All three intermingle, intermarry, sing to each other across their chicken wire fences, pull up roots and plant themselves inside each other's territory. A prose poem can be classified as a short short. A lyric essay as a prose poem. Lydia Davis's story "A Mown Lawn" was published in *Best American Poetry 2001*. Another story of hers appeared in D'Agata's collection of essays, where he *also* includes a sonnet cast in prose by James Wright ("May Morning," from *This Journey*). D'Agata points out that Wright's Petrarchan sonnet, like Richardson's ten-second essay, is in fact a poetic argument structured the same way a traditional five-paragraph essay is: thesis, elaboration upon that theme, evidence as example, and the conclusion or as he calls it, spin. The literary ecotone is a disorienting, dynamic, productive place, where the best pieces will survive only if they have made the most of the literary kingdoms they are surrounded by.

Beyond the structural, technical, and aesthetic choices a writer can make living along the edges of various genres, there is also the philosophical question common to all forms of art: do we favor an art that discovers brilliant, surprising connections between unlike things, or art that stubbornly insists that there are no connections, that chaos is the only law? This basic consideration underlies all the various hybrids we're discussing: is there buried order below all things, or disorder?

Returning briefly to the natural world, I'd like to close with a description of another edge species, the brown-headed cowbird, commonly found in forests, fields, and all habitats in between. The cowbird dispenses with a nest of its own, and instead, lays its eggs in the nests of other birds in forests, or near the forest edges.

Originally, cowbirds adopted this nestless habit to allow them to follow rambling bison herds, which kicked up insects upon which the birds fed. Now the female deposits as many as forty eggs in the nests of more than one hundred species. She sits around, watching patiently from a branch, or crashes through the woods to flush out the mother of a potential nest. She's picky and tends to go for nests with smaller eggs, swoops in at dawn and deposits one egg of her own. She sometimes evicts the other eggs by rolling them out with her beak, or even eats them, but mostly just lets nature take its course: the bigger mouth gets the better breakfast.

The more habitat disturbance, the more forests are plowed into fields, the more edge in relation to the forest interior, the better cowbirds do. Though some warblers have adjusted, ingeniously layering nest material over the cowbird's eggs, and their own and starting over—and some of these birds have been found with six-story nests—the cowbird remains an extremely successful resident of boundary zones.

So, if you find yourself perched along the edge between sea and land, keep your eyes peeled. And if you are considering the latest release, published perhaps by one of the more innovative independent presses, try to keep an open mind. Much of the new work in blended genres may irritate you or strike you as gimmicky. The air around you may be swarming with bugs and vegetation too thick to believe. But once in a while, if you are patient, you'll find a truly remarkable species in this wild and productive place we call *the edge*.

Chronicle
Sarah Blackman

He came as a mammal and I was mineral—a stalactite or a cluster of crystals at the bottom of a pond. All I was suggesting was form. Then, at the wedding, I was a fish and everyone could see me shimmer as I snuck away to smoke cigarettes and drink pink champagne. Or maybe it was the other way around. First I was a fish and then a mineral. First he was a stranger, then *this* man.

Behind the Wall
Alissa Nutting

I heard it first at night. Two squeaks, then a nibble. I stood on the bed fearing tiny fangs at my toes.

"It's coming from the wall," he said. "There are mice in the wall."

It's true, there were many, many mice. Over time I stopped hearing the yips and scratches. They became house-noises, full floorboards creaking.

Then one day I hung a picture. I felt handy in my heart. I wore a tool belt and was careful for my thumb.

"Thud," went the hammer, then "Squeak!"

I had nailed a picture and a mouse at the same time. It chirped loudly for a second, then not at all. I pictured it impaled and twitching, leaking blood onto untreated wood. If I removed the nail I would hear a plop. So I left it. I hung a photo of our wedding day.

Behind the wall, it is sinking to a wooly, grey fig. Soon there will be only bones. Soon the skeleton will lose its skin like hair, balding in patches that spread. The ribs will fall like china toothpicks, and I may hear the scrape of a pygmy chalkboard. The rattle of a miniature chime. I may scream in its delicate clank and curse all able ghosts.

The Space Between
Lia Purpura

> *Now, more than hitherto, there occurs shocks, surges, crossings, falls and almost scrambles, creating thus a different space, a space scattered and unknown, space enclosing spaces, superimposed, inserted, polyphonic perspectives.*
> —Henri Michaux

Where is the fear this afternoon? Where did it go and why can't I locate it now?

A goldfinch flies up while other leaves, gold and russety, sift and fall. A flight up, a flight down, the very air marked, so both rising and falling are held in a furor of sun-struck ongoingness.

I am outside this bright afternoon.

And even as I am built anew by fear these days, here, in Baltimore, I am also, right now, assembled by the brisk feel of New England, and fall, and my childhood there. That peace. Those biting blue skies. The elements mingle, brick by brick (though the sensation is softer and welling) and add up to this moment, a seep and twining that constitute *now*. Of course, this moment has little to do with simple construction, simple addition. But it's hard not to think in these terms.

I'll try again.

Events crosshatch: the air this afternoon is cleanly scented, still unstark, and in it, among sheering leaves, among goldfinches lifting and scalloping air, a sniper—in a patch of woods, gas station, mall parking lot—is hiding, aiming, and shooting.

And here, too, is the heavy sweater I'm wearing, thin at the elbows, the bruisy ferment of old apples, leaf dust, clouds stacked high in the west, *peace*.

Other things, too, are stacking up today: campaigns for Maryland's governor, though fewer of us now seem to notice, so frightened are we to pump gas, to let the children walk to school. *Candidates must wrest control of voter attention*, the paper says. "Rest," I say to my son, who learned from other kindergartners there's a bad person out there shooting, my son who's going to take it easy this afternoon, play Crazy Eights, maybe a little chess, inside.

Inside such perfect weather, an investigation is mounting. State Mounties are out on their horses, horses such as the angry men mounted this evening as they rode out of De Smet, Dakota Territories, to a riot at Stebbins camp, deep in Montana, 1878, I read to my son as he went uneasily to bed. As the Ingalls family rested uneasily *By the Shores of Silver Lake*, in the perpetual *now* that is book time. The children tucked in, the lake serene, the riot ongoing in moonlight, *on a night just like this*, I point out the window and up, to where "the great round moon hung in the sky and its radiance poured over a silvery world. Far, far away in every direction stretched motionless flatness, softly shining as if it were made of soft light." The moon outside Joseph's window. The very moon that swallowed both that writer's fear, and mine.

See how the moments go layering up?

These days, late afternoons in our small living room, a form unfurls and spreads its weave—music building and cloaking, uncloaking and reaching. The fugue my husband is working on makes available to light, and with a light of its own brings forth a moment: amber with its captured specks, bubbles of breath, and veering planes. And across the country, now, right now, in that other Washington, where it's a still-bright two in the afternoon, there's a search on for bullets a suspect once fired into a stand of trees. In a quiet neighborhood, ATF agents saw down stumps and haul them away in trucks as evidence.

Consider their find: cross-sectioned rings interrupted by bullets, all the loops of years pierced.

The loops of years pierced and containing the point.

This time of year, when the sky darkens early and clouds stack up in thick, western swells, I see therein a mountain range I once knew. (The sniper, we will come to learn, had a mount for his gun in the trunk of his car: the trunk of his car a small terrain of roughened upholstery, the gun at rest there, those beveled edges along the muzzle, the boredom of waiting, his fingernails scraping up curls of grime, flicking them off. Sun in a beam through the punched-out lock reaching a summit, casting its curves.)

Let me come back, though, to the matter at hand.

When the sky darkens and clouds rise like a near mountain range, my neighborhood plunges into a valley, makes of itself one of the small, snug towns I loved as a child in New England. I'd like you to believe, as I wanted to believe, that I actually "lived as a child in New England," for I felt such familiarity when visiting, as if I'd found a home I hadn't known I'd lost—in Great Barrington, East Hardwick, at our friends' small farm in Clarkesville, New Hampshire, way up near the Canadian border.

What it *is*—is what *else* it is. Not just that this afternoon's thick, boulder-clouds resemble the mountains I loved as a child, but that the one scene collapses in on the other, time reworks and folds together. And I live in both places.

What it is—is what else it is. For this reason I am often startled by the simplest gestures of things: a leaf scratching along sideways moves as a crab does, so much so that the animal's likeness comes powerfully in, and the shock of seeing a crab on the sidewalk trumps reason. And though I tell myself, "it's fall; *leaves* dry, scratch, and blow, not *crabs*," I'm jittery walking down the street—not frightened exactly, I can't say afraid—but always the scene I'm in breaks open and floods. The stuff of an *elsewhere* comes in, as when, among the dried, speckled shells of crabs this summer, a snowball rolled oceanward before returning itself to a clump of sea-foam. The flap of an awning blows in wind—and it's a low-flying bird's wing. The dark underside of a mushroom's gills, grown tiered and up-curved after rain, makes a tiny Sydney Opera House. Right there, hillside of the reservoir. Australia, just a few blocks from home.

I mean to say, too, that it's not all jittery, these exchanges. I remember seeing at my uncle's house, a cat's brain, preserved, and how the brain's topography slid into more: a crush of continents ribboning up, river-valleys gone to inclines, post-glacial, scoured and jarred. And how standing in front of the pen-and-ink drawings of neurons, those cells were stretching, wavering blooms, tributaries, sidewalk cracks.

Things pair up to go forth.

When I am clear enough to catch it, it's the motion of Bach's Prelude XIV, the sense of it-all-going-on-at-once, the voice seeding always the next swell, unending, the swell out-spinning, the strands of sound buoyant, a weave tightened and cinched like the lip of a purse until the last tilt, and the pucker of folds lets the gold go.

And my husband's sure fingers are cresting sound as they have moved over all that I am, and all I am overrun by.

I came across this a while ago: "In music the distance and the nearness of space, the limitless and the limited are all together in one gentle unity that is a comfort and a benefaction to the soul."

The space *a comfort.*

A *benefaction:*

And *what* in the soft air, the chalk-blue of the blue spruce, the sky orange and pink just the other morning as I took the garbage out—*what* ferried me past my fear? What brought me instead to my old summer job as a coffee vendor, Lower Manhattan, awake before dawn on Avenue C, the junkies cooled off, the Bowery wide and dank and mine to share with the bakery trucks, the newspaper trucks, just a few of us going out, a few coming home. Here's the blue dawn air settling over the cart I readied at my corner in front of Trinity Church, at Wall Street and Broadway—here now, in October, at 6:00 a.m, and fifteen years later.

What is it that took this morning over, washed it with a morning past and by that breath, kept from it the fear—who next will be shot?—also going on, right now. Right here.

Above this scene? Beyond it?

Where?

What about this, from Emerson's journal: "The universe is a more amazing puzzle than ever, as you glance along this bewildering series of animated forms—the hazy butterflies, the carved shells, the birds, beasts, fishes, insects, snakes, the upheaving principle of life everywhere incipient, in the very rock aping organized forms. Not a form so grotesque, so savage, nor so beautiful but is an expression of some property inherent in man the observer, an occult relation between the very scorpions and man. I feel the centipede in me, cayman, carp, eagle and fox. I am moved by strange sympathies."

Strange, yes, this sympathy, clearing a space, preparing a ground for meetings to occur—but fragile, too. Terribly fragile. So why, *why,* I have been wondering, did my friend, standing at the shore one night this summer, watching the white breakers arc, curl, and fall—why did she say, even as the chill spray hit our faces and we shivered in relief from the day's heat, *how* could she say, "It's just like a movie"? And pull us from the evening damp, the woody, splintered boardwalk, sweet ache of leaning on the chest-high railing, rumble of the arcade fading, folding in and out of wind? Why break the hum and echo of the moment we were in? Why leave the moment just then forming, moment that would, some morning, some evening, return to her a quality of light or air or scent to displace the sadness she might be feeling?

I've never been able to conjure, in winter, summer's heat. I cannot, by will, regard the snow into a fringe of green. So while I believe the sniper will be caught, I cannot summon that peace, nor compose a time without this pulse of fear. I only know fear comes to me. And also peace.

On October 24, hours before dawn, the sniper is caught, with an accomplice, sleeping at a rest stop near Myersville, Maryland. It's been twenty-five days now since the rampage began. Eleven people are dead. And though the snipers are locked far from us now, a world away—three miles away, just downtown, in hyperbolized space (Supermax, the *sine qua non* of desolation)—*here* they still are, large in their absence, some place, circling. Fall, like an axis, collected them in, spooled all the fear up.

Fall also spun around itself translucing yellows and flaming red stems. Last flocks lifting whole into trees for a rest, leafing back the empty spots, and late afternoons, a neighbor's carrier pigeons let out for a spin, angling like a single wing, an arm crooked up to block the glare. Thick pumpkins. White mums. Fall gathered these in.

And fall gathered, too, on this afternoon, my husband working up Prelude XIV; my son and his friends dropping split, rotting walnuts, *thunk,* in tin pails; the blade of air sharpening as the temperature falls; box elder bugs swarming the shed's southern wall—and everything, everything else uncountable, unaccountably part of, that constitutes *now*. And all this I call *fall,* I call *late afternoon,* will come back, will come hauling its wedge of cold fear, its unbidden relief, oh who can know which, some long summer hour when lines of road tar loosen in heat, a boy sits idly peeling a stick, and wood wasps drill slow, perfect circles in eaves.

Imagining Bisbee
Alicita Rodríguez

Few people live in Bisbee; the town's history makes it so. When miners decided to strike in 1917, the sheriff's deputies, with their big guns and small teeth, rounded them up like cattle, packed them into train cars, and shipped them to New Mexico—dumped the strikers, with their soot-covered faces, smack in the middle of desert. A few of the miners walked back to Bisbee, each step, each raising and dropping of the foot taken amidst a jumble of hallucinations. These are the forefathers.

And so, their progeny.

Bisbee Bob, drug dealer, father of two suspected arsonists.

Walking Bob, Francophile, tours the Côte d'Azur each summer, raves about the country's footpaths.

Bible Bob, eighty years old, thin as a pencil, eats only carrots, skin hangs in folds, scribbles in notebooks, recognizable by red rubber raincoat.

Crazy Nancy, bright lipstick, black hair, junkie. Reportedly a brutal suicide.

Library Girl, reads, looks for forest fires with *perro callejero*.

Built into the mountains, Bisbee is a town of steps. Natives decorate their steps in many ways. Some string colored electric lights along the treads. The more creative choose novelty bulbs in the shape of bumblebees or cactus trees or cowboy boots. Others paint the risers with bright colors; some imitate the designs of the surrounding Indian tribes. Still others paste tiny pieces of broken glass onto the stairs. The paths to their homes glisten and blind in the Arizona sun.

Bisbee's inhabitants want to disappear. They use PO boxes and first names. They hide under straw hats and melt into the horizon. They don't see movies and they only sleep with foreigners. They never get biblical with one another.

Ecotone: reimagining place

It is a town that exists only in relation to other realities: south of Tombstone; east of Nogales; north of Mexico; west of the Arizona/New Mexico border. Bisbee often does not appear on maps. It is not there.

Across the Broad Hills, 1885
Claudia MonPere

Sky thick with rain,
land rich for grazing: sagebrush,
brome, red stem filigree.

My lambs grow fat.
Shy white spots
bunched around Jacalitos Creek.

Lollie pours drinks at the Santa
Fe Basque Hotel. I do my
talking with the wind.

Thin, silver,
my words pipe into the canyon.
The sheep graze. Weeks

flow through me. No one
but a ring of bandits
hunched around my fire

one night. We drink,
play some hands of Mus.
You are mine, I call

to the land I don't own.
They spill from my dreams,
seventeen gutted sheep.

Maki barked into the trees.
Still the lions hunted.

Yes, I am only a tramp

sheepman. My greasy
tent, my hobbling burro.
My lambs, my lambs.

Squirrel
Patrick Phillips

The day my brother
got that .22
the pellet gun was mine:

mine to load
and mine to hold,
mine to love

a little more each time
I shut one eye
and turned to stone—

aiming so high into the leaves
my pulse
blinked off and on.

We killed more
than the day was long,
then gutted them for skins.

And I forgot,
from then till now,
that feeling in my hands

as my brother in his shades
said *shit*, and *bitch*,
and called me *Little Man*.

Walden
SETH HARWOOD

Noah Bennett didn't know the right thing to do. He and Corinne had just broken up, something that felt right, but he couldn't be sure.

After a hard year apart, trying to navigate the difficulties of a long-distance relationship, Noah had come back to Boston for the summer break from his MBA classes at Northwestern. They had both come to recognize that spending their summer together was critical. If they never saw each other, what was the point? So Noah moved back to Boston, into Corinne's small apartment where everything was tastefully decorated in light colors and floral prints from where she'd grown up in the south of France. In Chicago, he could have lined up an internship with any of a half-dozen brokerage houses, but in Boston the job searching went slowly. After two weeks of interviews that led to nothing, he began to realize that spending his days alone in Corinne's apartment, waiting for interviews or for her to come home, was not what he wanted.

They started talking at five that morning, after she found him awake in the living room, watching the sunrise. When she came in, Noah didn't look. "I can't do this anymore," he said. "I wish I could, but I can't."

"What is wrong with this?" she asked. "We were going to try."

"I know," he said. "But it's not right. That's the best I can explain. I wish it was another way." On the other side of the street, one of the thin pipes atop a large brick building emitted a trail of steam that rose up into the sky. "I'm sorry."

She called in sick. He wished she wouldn't, but she was crying, hard, and wanted to help him pack his things. Noah left—he had to get out of the apartment; he went to Cambridge to get his mother's car, but Corinne was still there when he got back, which made packing even harder. She refused to do anything but help him, a kindness he could barely endure, and together they turned the morning into a series of crying and ruined goodbyes.

When the car was packed, he went to his mother's. His father was there, waiting to talk to him, to find out what his plans were. Noah told him the relationship had come to a permanent-feeling close, that he felt like he'd finally made an important decision. It felt *right*, he told his father.

Then, in the late afternoon, Corinne called him. "I've just been laid off," she whispered over the phone. "I don't have a job."

"Jesus," he said, sitting alone in what had once been his bedroom at his mother's, the room where he had once punched a man named Vaughn—a boyfriend of his mother's whom Noah had thought she should not date.

Now, he held the phone close to his head and looked at his suitcase on the other side of the room. He closed his eyes. "How did this happen?" he asked.

"They said they have to make cutbacks," she said. "Jana told me they're laying off six people." She said she wasn't even supposed to show up to work tomorrow; they'd told her today had been her last.

"I thought they had to give you two weeks," he said. He had been back from Chicago for less than a month. "Do you want me to come over?"

She did. "I want to," he said. Of course he should go. He felt guilty for offering in a way that forced her to ask. He would see her, that was what made the most sense; he would go there, set himself aside and go because she needed him. He could push his decisions away for tonight, at least.

He found his parents in the backyard talking, behaving like friends, for once. When Noah told them what had happened, they couldn't believe it. "That's *terrible*!" his father said.

"I know. I'm going over there. That's the right thing to do, right?"

They shrugged. His father always pushed him to make his own decisions, avoided offering advice. But he knew to go. His mother told him to take the car, even gave him money to spend on dinner. He thought eating something would help, and so he called ahead to order ribs and chicken, the best thing he could think of at a time like this. But he hoped Corinne would eat.

She looked under control when she came down to open the door. He set the bags of food down and hugged her, wrapped her in his arms, and held her shoulders. "It'll all be all right," he said. "Things will turn around. You'll get past this."

When she straightened, he asked her if they should eat in the courtyard, or upstairs in her apartment. She said downstairs was where Jana had told her. "She wasn't sure how to. She told me one of the principals wanted to come, that she had thought to bring Katia, but finally decided to come alone." Noah knew that Jana lived close by, that she and Corinne were friends, went to brunch occasionally. "She just came here and told me they were letting me go."

"And it's effective today?" She wiped her fingers under her eyes, nodding. "What did you say?"

"I told her I just wanted to go upstairs and be alone."

She led him into the elevator. They had ridden in this small compartment many times, holding hands, kissing, even taking off each others' clothes one night, drunk, coming in past midnight. Now they stood apart from one another, and Noah's hands held only white plastic bags of white Styrofoam containers.

They got off on her floor and he followed her down the hall, the one he'd been so impressed by the first time he'd seen it. Looking at her welcome mat, the flowered design distinctly hers, he smiled. In her apartment, he could still feel the heavy effects of the day's heat weighing down on them, on the air. It was only July, but the day felt like mid-August.

Noah went out to the apartment's thin balcony, hoping for a breeze, and started setting the food on the small iron table. He brought out the two new folding chairs Corinne had just bought. He'd known two would be unnecessary soon, but had kept quiet because he hadn't wanted to rush. Now he set the chairs on the sides of the table and started unwrapping the food. They had Cokes, coleslaw, chicken, ribs, macaroni and cheese, candied yams, collard greens. All of it smelled good.

"Eating is a good thing at a time like this," he said. "It can make you feel better, even if only a little." He tasted the macaroni. "Here, this is good," he said. She came to the door and he handed her the container. She looked uninterested, tasted a small bite, and passed it back. Noah could not ignore the ribs and he started eating—he was suddenly very hungry. He was glad to see her come outside and sit down across from him, but she just sat there, looking at the street below. He kept eating, hoping she'd relax, and he was holding a rib, with barbecue sauce all over his hands, when he looked up and saw her crying. He wiped his hands on some napkins and reached for her, but in the awkward folding chair and across the table, he only could manage his hand onto her knee. "Oh, Bear," he said.

She dried her eyes with her fingers. "It's not fair. I've been doing a good job. That's what everyone tells me. Why would they do this?"

"I'm sorry," he said. He wiped his mouth. "Let's go inside. Can we?" He wanted to hold her and let her cry this thing out, for things to be all right. He led her inside and onto the couch, abandoning the food. He sat with his arm across her shoulders. "How did this happen?" he asked. He leaned back and gently guided her down with him, helped her to lie on his chest.

"My father said I should come home," she said, putting her head against his shoulder. "I could hear my mother crying. They both said I should come home. That's their answer."

He touched her hair with his fingers and put his other arm around her back. "It's a lot to move halfway around the world from where you grew up. Maybe it would be nice to go back to Arles for a while, just to relax and let this thing blow over. You wouldn't have to stay long."

"No," she said. "I'm not ready to do that. Not now." She leaned into him and then sat up, wiping her face with her hands. He saw the food outside, the bags blowing in the wind, and got up to bring the containers inside. He set them on the coffee table.

"Here," he said, unwrapping the chicken and tasting a bite. "This is good. Try this. I think if you eat something you'll start feeling better."

"It just doesn't feel right to leave. There are other US cities I want to try. New York."

"This gives you the chance then, right?" He wrapped the food and put it in the kitchen, washed his hands, and came back to the couch. "Think of this as though you just got two free months to really think about where you want to go next, a summer vacation. You can find a new job, take time to think things over, figure out what you want." She nodded and he worked his hand up her back. He massaged the twin tendons in her neck, feeling their tension, then worked around and down to her shoulder blades and along the sides of her back with both hands.

"Now that I don't have a job I could come with you to Chicago," she said.

He looked out the window and thought of that morning: how he'd felt sitting on the couch, thinking, when he couldn't sleep. The day had moved on, but the buildings across the street, and his feelings, were the same. "I don't know," he said. "Maybe it's still not right for us. Maybe we still have to try something different."

"I know," she said. Her breath evened out, slowed. He handed her the tissues and she blew her nose, then he took her in his arms and lay back again. He held her on his chest, rocking slightly; she brought her legs up onto the couch.

"This is big, Bear," he said. "But some day you might look back and think how it made you stronger." He listened to her breathe, watching the clouds shift outside her windows. "I know that sounds stupid," he said.

He still loved to hold her. Sometimes at night he had imagined a world where their bed was everything and he could save her from the difficulties of life, just by keeping her there in his arms, but lately it had been just their two bodies on her hard futon, trying to sleep in the heat, her warmth making him uncomfortable. Perhaps it was her metabolism that made her body so hot—she liked her shower water scalding, always said she felt cold. Her body kept their bed warm like an oven.

She slid her fingers along the inside of his forearm and he moved it away from her. In a rush, what had troubled him about their relationship came back to him: it was about simple touches like that one, things he wanted to tell her and couldn't, about how they never seemed completely capable of expressing their feelings to one another. He remembered the time he'd tried to tell her why he didn't like her to touch the soft inside of his wrist, and how she'd started crying. He closed his eyes.

"We should do something," he said, helping her up. "Maybe we could go for a walk?" He doubted if anything could make her happy. "We could go to Newbury."

That she sat up and agreed surprised him; she seemed almost pleased, as if going were actually a good idea. Newbury Street had been a place where they'd eaten fancy dinners the summer before, shopped and bought expensive clothes they thought they could afford. But even then, over nice food, *something* had seemed wrong to him. Even then.

Now he would drive them to Newbury Street in his mother's car. It would be good to drive; after two months of living with Corinne and riding everywhere in her car, he missed feeling in control, even of something so small.

He held her waist as they walked to the elevator and they held hands outside as they walked to the car. "It's hot tonight," he said. "Today was like the first hot humid day of summer, and we made it. *You* made it. You got through one of the worst days I've ever heard of today. That was a lot, Bear."

She nodded. "I hope you'll always call me that."

"And it's still hot," he said. She had her hand inside the crook of his elbow and he maneuvered his way out to wrap his arm around her back. "We should go swimming. How about we go out to Walden Pond?"

"Really," she said, her face suddenly bright. She turned toward him, took both of his hands. "Can we?"

He knew how difficult it would be to go: it was a long drive that cooled you off as you drove there, the water was always cold, and sneaking in could be difficult—but now they had to try it. She was as happy as he'd seen her all night. "Let's go, then," he said. "Let's drive out there."

She was smiling now. "Okay," she said. "Good. We're going to Walden Pond."

At a small sidewalk café outside her apartment, a trio played jazz. Noah noticed a young couple with short dreadlocks sitting on a nearby wooden bench, listening. Their arms were entwined and they held hands, each of them tapping out time to the music with their feet. There were other couples sitting at the café's fancy tables, but these two sat apart, quietly enjoying the night, smiling, not worried about how they appeared to the others. They seemed happy, and Noah envied them for this. He wondered how they had come to find one another or what it took to feel comfortable like that, a way he had never felt with Corinne, with anyone.

He opened her door at the car, glad to be helping, doing something for her after the two full months of her helping him. He wanted to do *something* that could make her feel better, that was all he wanted, to do this for her, help her to end this night. As they drove along the Charles, he saw the familiar sights he had always loved: the Boston skyline, the Citgo sign, the fancy Back Bay apartments with the big windows that you could see into—the ones he imagined owning some day, looking out onto the river and Storrow Drive. He was glad he had come home to try living with her: nothing had been lost, he reasoned, and now he could say he had given it a legitimate try.

She stayed quiet until they got to the highway, then, with trees on both sides, she spoke of growing up in France, how beautiful the mountains and the forests were there. She told him that these suburbs outside of Boston, their tree-covered rolling hills and the nice cars, reminded her of home. And he knew that he still loved her. It pained him as he listened to her voice, as she held his hand. He wanted to do anything to help her get over this, even though he knew the water in the pond would be cold.

In Concord, he checked the front gate and found it locked as he'd expected, but there were a few cars parked by the Thoreau Gift Shop. He couldn't remember if he'd ever seen cars there at night before. But there they were. If someone watched these spots they might ticket him, but probably wouldn't tow—he hoped not.

"Do you think it'd be all right for us to park here?" he asked.

"I don't know. We won't be long, will we?"

"No," he said. "You're right."

He parked and locked his door, then went around to her side. She was still inside, looking through her purse, and he tapped on her window. "We should go," he said. "It'd be bad if anyone saw us here." He looked at the other cars to see if any of them had a common identifier, any sign of some group designation, but none did. The car next to his was a station wagon with Missouri plates, a road atlas spread across the front seat, two sleeping bags in the back.

The air here was much cooler and less thick than in the city; the humidity was gone—the trees and the pond seemed to cool everything—but Noah had the air-conditioning off and the windows closed on the ride out, so they were still sticky from the city, warm enough to swim.

"It's *so* nice here," she said.

He took her hand and led her toward the entrance. It was dark, and the quiet of the empty forest brought back its familiar spookiness. They crouched under the gate, going separately, but rejoined hands after, at the top of the downhill slope of a road. They climbed down, passing under trees in darkness, and emerged onto a beach lit by the moonlight. "It's wonderful," she said, walking to the water, bending to feel it. "And so warm."

He directed her to a trail that led to the more secluded spots farther along the shoreline. At the trailhead, trees crowded in on both sides, the heavy forest sloping above, dark and full of sounds, and a thin line of pines between them and the pond. He could hear the sound of water lapping gently against the shore.

She walked ahead, taking the trail like she knew it, as he held back, keeping track of the wire fence that protected the shore, looking for an opening where they could swim. "The air is so clear and clean here," she said.

In a few minutes, his eyes had adjusted to the darkness, but he could not see the water when he heard a panting, splashing sound ahead of them, and he grabbed her hand. "Shhh. There's something there," he said. If it was an animal, he didn't want it to surprise them, but he didn't want to surprise it either. He went ahead of her, slowly, feeling along the wire, chilled by the oddness of this sound. In the dark, his imagination always convinced him that sounds were made by creatures. Some *thing* must be in the water.

"I think it's—" she said, and she started laughing.

At a break in the fence, he saw steps leading down to the water with people's clothes set in piles. He realized that he'd heard a woman. She was just getting used to the cold water, breathing hard and splashing around. Corinne laughed. "It's all right here, Noah," she said, walking ahead again. "Don't be afraid."

As he followed, he felt along the fence for another break, hoping to find an empty set of steps to the water. They followed the path as it wrapped around a long bend of shoreline, approaching the far beaches he liked to come to in the summer. And then, when he found the next gap in the fence, the dark stones leading down were empty of clothes and they were separated from the other people by the bend; no one else was around. He saw water splashing against the shore. "This is our spot," he said.

She stopped, leaning forward to see, and said, "Perfect."

He stepped down and took her hand to help her down. He wanted to sweep her legs into his arms and carry her, but he didn't, knew he would never do something like that here, that if he fell while carrying her down the steep stones they'd both be badly hurt. Instead, he took each step ahead of her and held her hand as she lowered herself behind him.

Tonight she wore the old clothes that had been his favorite those first long weekends after he met her at his cousin's wedding, when he flew in for visits: her long blue skirt fanned out around her feet, his favorite Nikes, and her tank top that fit her as tightly as anything she owned. She held the skirt above her knees with one hand so she could step freely down the stairs, and he saw her legs from her small blue sneakers up—her legs that were always perfectly shaven. He wanted to touch them, to run his fingers along her smooth calves. But instead he lowered himself down the steps to where only the pond was below him. Careful to hold her arm until her feet were steady, he sat and hugged her legs, feeling her shin with his fingers. "What do you think, Bear?"

"It's beautiful here. The pond, its ripples, and the moon's reflection, all the stars. It's so wonderful."

"Yeah," he said. "I hope the water's not too cold."

"You're so grumpy," she said. "You've always been sad."

He placed his shoes on the step above him, took his shirt off, and stretched his toes to the water. It was cold, but he tried saying, "It's not so bad." They had come this far. "I've been here at night before," he said, "But always later in the summer. There haven't been *that* many warm days yet."

He slid off the rock, into the shallow water, and landed on soft sand. "Yow," he said. "It's *pretty* cold."

"You're not going to swim in your shorts, are you?" she asked.

He looked down at himself, knowing that he still had shorts on. "No," he said. "I was just feeling the water." He heard the people they'd passed, the gentle splashing of the man and the woman, but he couldn't see any movement or shapes along the shoreline in the dark. He unbuttoned his shorts and, careful not to lose his wallet or keys, stepped out of them one leg at a time, holding them above the water.

She touched his shoulder, steadying herself for balance as she removed her shoes.

He folded his shorts and put them on the step next to her, naked in an unfamiliar, unembarrassed way. His penis stood out below his stomach, but he was not ashamed of how the moonlight revealed it. The water cold on his ankles, he was here, with her, and for the first time everything seemed fine. He told himself everything *was* fine.

She stood above him in the moonlight and slipped out of her skirt. Her body looked as beautiful as he'd ever seen it, her legs long and pale, a simple white thong, which she slipped down over her feet, onto the stones. When she pulled the top over her head, her nipples pointed in the cold. He saw the flatness of her stomach, thought how her body was as perfect as any he'd ever known, with a realness that was fully human—she had bones under her skin. He stood below her, beholding the simple beauty of the pond and the trees around them, and her bright pale form above him. She shone in the moonlight, illuminated as if the moon for that moment had focused its brilliance on her. She stood no less than three feet above him, nude, shining. The shadow of a tree branch cut across her side. He followed its curve to her breast with his eyes, thinking as if his gaze were his fingers. He passed over her shoulders, along the line of her collarbone, and up her white neck. When he came to her eyes, she smiled as if she knew the moon had caught her this way, given her such light.

"We're at Walden Pond," she said and laughed.

He heard the wind and felt a cold gust prickling the hair on his legs, making his skin tighter. After a chill ran through him, he touched her leg, felt its smoothness. She giggled. "You're beautiful," he said. He held his hand up for her to take it and when she did he steadied her and she bent down to step into the water. "It's only sand here," he said. "Don't worry."

As she crouched and slipped her leg down, she laughed at the touch of the cold on her toes, squeezed his hand. When her left foot fell onto the sand, she slipped slightly so that she landed suddenly with both feet in the water, both of her hands on his shoulders to steady herself.

"Ha. It's not so bad, then," she said. "This can be our baptism. Where we wash it all away and start fresh, promising ourselves that from here on nothing bad will happen to us. That we'll wash it all away and leave only the best things."

"But some of what happened today won't change." He was sorry as soon as he'd said it, but he wanted everything to remain clear.

"I know," she said. "But this will clean us, this can change *something*, even if only for us as separate people." She caught her breath as the water hit her thighs. "Only good things will happen after this for us. Let's promise." Her voice was soft. She put her hand on his arm and he noticed her eyes were closed. "We can wash away the bad luck and whatever is hard, and come to something new."

"Okay," he said. She led him out into the cold water. "I promise," he told her, stepping forward, wading deeper until the water reached his shins, then his knees and—too quickly, it seemed—the tops of his thighs. The water was clean and cold, pure. "You deserve good things," he said. "They'll come to you."

"We're washing everything bad away."

His penis seemed to be floating above the pond, standing erect on its own. She looked at it and smiled. "I see you," she said, and reached out to touch him.

He stepped forward. "Co-o-o-ld," he said. "This is where it hurts."

He stepped into deeper water, breathing like a Lamaze student, fighting the shock. She laughed. "You're brave." He raised his hand to splash her, but realized how out of the question that was—an act for a summer day, with the sun hot on their skin.

Now *he* led *her* deeper, until he was in to his sternum and she to her shoulders, and she was shivering, shaking in the water. She swam in front of him and stood against his chest, her teeth chattering, their bodies together. When he touched her shoulder, she shied away, but then held him when he took her in his arms. He ran his hand along her legs, feeling the goosebumps on her skin, and brought them up, around his waist. He felt surprise at how warm her body seemed against his; she was warmer than him, warming him in the cold water. He held his arms along the backs of her thighs, supporting her as she grasped him by the shoulders, her legs around his waist.

"It's *so* cold," she said, her hair wet against his neck.

"You're keeping me warm, Bear. Your oven."

She kissed his neck and her lips were cold, but she'd stopped shivering. He pressed her against him and carried her out until the water was at his neck—where only his feet could touch the bottom—and he did not feel cold.

"We're in," she said. "We made it."

"Because of you."

She kissed his forehead and his temple; their lips met and he could feel hers cold and soft, moving as she told him she loved him, and then they finally kissed, the tip of her tongue warm between his lips. Her legs had smoothed but her nipples stood erect against his chest. He nuzzled his face into her shoulder, holding her tight to his chest for her warmth, squeezing her.

The cold water occurred to him as if it was only a fact now; he discerned its clean film against him, but she staved off his feeling the cold.

"We're clean," she said.

The moon and the Big Dipper hung above them; the trees along the opposite shore reflecting darkness against the still water of the pond. He felt held: by her, by the water, and as if the crispness *had* done something to him, something he could not explain. He wondered how many more times he would hold her body, if he ever would again, and he thought about times he'd held her: in a hotel room on a vacation in Barcelona, after she'd flown all night to see him; the night after his grandmother died, when he'd counted the beating of their hearts; and after their first time together, when he peeked under the covers and secretly looked at her body.

Then, from somewhere in the world beyond the trees, he heard the rumble and the whistle of a train coming, and soon he saw the lights and the cars themselves skirting along the top edge of the pond, just behind the tree line in the woods. He turned so she could see it. "It's a train," he said.

It was headed away from them, taking strangers to their homes in the night—places he might never see, places inhabited by people he'd never know.

It rattled on its tracks, a line of a dozen passenger cars knocking along in the night. The rush of it speeding away toward destinations he would never take her to—places he would have to explore on his own—this chilled him. He couldn't move until the train was gone. Then, when it had passed, they stood and listened. Her body felt clean and smooth; she held her lips cold against his neck, and the wet ends of her hair brushed his cheek. She squeezed herself against his body. He smoothed her hair back, cupping her head in his hands.

He kissed her then, felt the cold slipperiness of her lips and the sharpness of her tongue moving against his. Her eyelashes tickled his cheeks. Her lips were dark from the cold. She looked cleaned, *cleansed*, and he believed it, believed in her. They kissed again, and, though he knew it was time to go, he held her more tightly. He felt the protection of her legs around him and her warmth against his chest, the comfort from the cold that he'd never expected, and he *knew*: he knew what it would mean to be alone.

Who Needs Nature?
Julianna Baggott

My mother despised nature. Boy Scouts on camping trips seemed suicidal—my God, the poison ivy, the humming mosquitoes with their full tanks of disease. Why take your lives in your hands, gentlemen? She raised me to fear all greenery, all wild animals—even squirrels and frogs. (Squirrels can be rabid. Frogs can pee on you and cause warts.) My mother said things like: What's wrong with communing with nature from a screened-in porch? Why do we have to go traipsing through it to feel alive? My mother has always felt plenty alive—her nervous system set to overdrive. She shakes with life. Her voice—always under a bit of pressure—can still call out with more vitality—if not high-pitched panic—than all other mothers I know combined.

My father had been raised in the mountains of West Virginia. He loved nature. He sang John Denver songs at the top of his lungs. He longed to be in the great outdoors. He was, however, a corporate lawyer who spent most of his hours in a stuffy office, yanking at his neckties. (But he was otherworldy. He was living another life in his rich mind, which is why his shiny business shoes often didn't match—one blacker and more worn than the other. Also, he often dressed in the dark so my mother could sleep in.) When he drove past cows bowed to fields, he often leaned out of the window, banged on the roof of the car, and mooed to them—as if he understood, deeply, what it was to be penned up.

Every summer, my father took us on vacation to a place called Lost River—somewhere in West Virginia, a row of log cabins built during the WPA in the thirties, running up mountainous terrain. My mother allowed it only because my father would truly relax there. He would even sleep in himself, and she worried about his health. She worried about most everything.

I hated the place—the crappy nature film they replayed each Monday night for decades, the sub-zero swimming pool, the tiny gift shop filled with small cedar boxes with the words "Lost River" printed on them, and then there was the fact that there was no river at Lost River at all. It was lost. I could appreciate that they weren't trying to hide the lack of a river, but still it struck me as all wrong—like the park had suffered a river lobotomy and decided to boast about it.

Unlike me, my mother was relieved that there was no river—as that would have only led to dangerous swimming, fear of pollution, and water snakes. There were trees everywhere, leafy green plants—all of which looked like poison ivy to her—wild mushrooms and berries that children were likely to pop into their mouths and then die from. There were varmints, mosquitoes, ticks, and bats. Not far off, there were bears and wolves. And on top of all of that, there was no washing machine, no dishwasher—nothing to scald the germs.

I objected to the gnats which swarmed in clumps on the shabby croquet field punctuated by dented wickets. The gnats gunned for me. I had oversized eyes as a child. I still do, somewhat, though my face has grown into them a bit. My child eyes were so big on my face that gnats used to mistake my eyes for ponds and try to congregate there. My eyes were dive-bombed by gnats—bejeweled by gnats. My father—at the tail end of the Hankie Generation—used to take his hankie from his back pocket, twist its tip with a bit of spit, and dig out the gnats. The gnats only further proved my mother's point: that the natural world is no place for human beings.

I couldn't swim in the swimming pool for more than a few minutes before turning blue. I was extremely skinny. My mother fed me constantly. I refused to fatten. I was her failure. Death was all around us, certainly, and not only because of nature. It lurked in the germy folds of our lives. And yet one thing she could be sure of was that her children wouldn't lack nutrition. Except that it seemed like I did. On these vacations we met up with my aunts and uncles and cousins. They were fond of saying, "So doesn't your mother feed you?" Ha ha. These cracks jacked my mother's neuroses. She took them personally. My mother was exasperated. "She eats and eats! You should see her!"

And I did. I ate and ate and ate—especially in front of relatives. In fact, I still eat extremely well in front of others. I imagine my eating well—at a nice dinner party—sets the anxious guests at ease—as if, like my mother, my food intake were a major concern. I can't help it. I imagine them blaming my mother and, by eating, I'm releasing her of any responsibility, clearing her name.

Because I was so skinny, my mother worried over me more than the other children. She feared that I had a disease that hadn't yet been named. She didn't want me to be put in any perilous situations—and nature hikes could be perilous—and so on these vacations, I often stayed in the cabin with her, playing cards. And while we played cards, my mother told me stories.

It isn't surprising then that what I recall most from Lost River isn't the gnats or the freezing pool or the nature film or the nature itself, which I didn't participate in. What I remember most is stories—not stories of my childhood, but of my mother's family. It's as if I were a blank slate, but instead of my own experience written there, my mother—and later my father—had the chalk and filled in with their own pasts. This seems a little strange to me. I know that most people think back on their youthful obsession with things like comic book heroes or Shaun Cassidy or horses or a collection of 45s or the Red Sox. But I filled up on Southern gothic lore.

It was in the cabin at Lost River where my mother told me the story that reached the farthest back in our family's mythology. The mythology of my mother's family begins with archetype—as good myths do. It's been handed down, worn through, to some essential first. A vague knot. One small bone. The eye tooth of what once was a full body of a story—that's all that's left. The cabin at Lost River was the best place to hand this story over. My mother may have despised the cabin and the woods that surrounded it with gracious offerings of death, but she knew that these elements were useful. They added to the atmosphere—our people could have lived in a cabin similar to this, in woods like these.

The story goes like this:

A young man and a young woman and a baby were leaving home on a horse. There was a storm, and the mother and the father and the horse were killed. But the baby lived, found, days later, wrapped in a grapevine—alive.

And that was my ancestor. The baby found in the grapevine. A girl baby? A boy baby? A true story? A myth found in many cultures the world over? The grapevine gives it a biblical feel. The young man and woman and child on a horse—again biblical. Were they leaving their family? Were they desperate? Why else head out in a storm? Did the horse have to die too? Wasn't that a little gratuitous? No matter. The defining element of the story was this: the baby was a survivor. We hail from a survivor, and, prior to that, people who get pissed off enough to try to leave town in the middle of a storm.

I loved the story. I suddenly loved the cabin and the woods. I wanted to go out and stalk around and find a grapevine. I was a lonesome kid, in a way, if you can be a lonesome kid with a brother and two sisters. They would be gone by the time I was nine by this point and when I turned eleven, they'd be gone already, living their own lives. I needed the stories that my mother told me, and my mother needed to tell them. She was going through menopause. She was emotional, easily pulled in by the undertow of memory. I listened to that story. I soaked it in. I accepted it as a gift, as love. And so this is where I accepted the principle that giving stories is giving love, and listening to stories is accepting love. The result? A naïve confusion that led to a life of conflicted relationships with critics? A truth—because perception is reality? Maybe it's an equation that everyone has to make for themselves. Frankly, I could have done worse than story = love—for example: toy = love, cookie = love, sexual perversion = love, heroin = love.

And speaking of love, my mother let me go off with my father on the next hike. She didn't want to, but she consented. I was coated in insect repellent and suntan lotion and wore a hat. We packed a lunch and set out in the morning. We walked to a farm where we rented horses, and we rode a trail up to a lookout called Cranny Crow. We took pictures at the lookout. We took pictures with our horses. We called out off of the mountain and let it echo down into the valley below. And I rode the old trail horse and thought of my ancestors leaving home. I thought of the baby and the wind and the gathering clouds. I thought of the dark settling in around them and the first drops of rain, heavy and fat, ticking in the trees around them.

After dinner that night, my mother gave me a head check for ticks under the bulb in the bathroom. I failed. A fat tick had embedded itself in my scalp.

"Did you wear your hat?" she asked.

"Most of the time," I said. Had my ancestors worn fishing-style hats with wide brims that slipped down over their eyes? No. I'd taken mine off as soon as I'd gotten on the horse. I wanted to feel every bit of breeze in my hair.

My mother cried out for my father, "Bill, Bill! Come quick!"

And there was my father in the doorway, at-the-ready. He loved

Lost River—the mountains of his youth, the distressed cabins, the notion that for one week of the year we were living right—a family of pioneers. But he understood how hard it was for my mother. He knew that she was trying her damnedest, that these vacations felt like punishment for her.

My mother hurriedly gathered peroxide and tweezers—she was always prepared. She combined aspirin bottles so that she would have one empty container to save the tick for later examination by a doctor, if it turned out to be a foul one. She handed the tweezers to my father. He was in charge of all things surgical and bug-related. My father dug the tick from my head—its body first. He dropped it into the bottle—and then excavated its more stubbornly rooted head. He screwed on the lid of the aspirin bottle. My mother poured peroxide on the barren spot on my head. It fizzed and stung. My older brother and sisters continued to play Uno at a card table. My father rejoined them.

I got in bed. My mother pulled a chair into the room. She wrote the date on the tick jar and sat it on the desk beside her. She watched over me, checking her wristwatch. She was waiting for signs of fever, headache, kidney failure, shock. I imagined rabies: myself lockjawed, foaming at the mouth. I kept an eye on my mother, keeping an eye on me—big-eyed, skinny, my head, fizzing with peroxide, filled up on story. Throughout my childhood, my mother hovered and I hovered back—battle after battle of a Hovering War.

She told me the bedtime story of a football coach who'd recently died from Rocky Mountain Spotted Fever. He'd been famous, and then the tick bit him, and he died. "But you'll be fine," she told me. "Go to sleep. I'm here."

And I believed her. I understood the world was a dangerous place, but I was lucky. My mother was the keeper of all stories, she knew all dangers, and her watchful love would save us all.

Things got quiet—except for the tick, miraculously alive.

"It's amazing how long ticks can live," my mother whispered, "headless in a bottle with no air."

"Survivors," I said. Like us, I meant. Like us and the baby in the grapevine!

"That's right," my mother said.

The tick was going to die, of course. But that wasn't the point of the survival metaphor right now, and if it were, then the tick was going to die because it didn't have a mother like my mother—so loving, so generous, so watchful. And we listened to the tick—headless, airless—clicking around the bottom of the aspirin bottle. And I fell asleep before it stopped.

Inerrancy
David Wright

An engine again like a belly that won't fill.

The hunger after a day of hard work we've completed,
                                        unsatisfactory, finished—
the requirements. What were we asked to do in the first place,
what needed fixing or building? Over the mechanical rumble a pack
                                        of boys
owns the sidewalk, their bodies announcing energy, fists and limbs
                                        coiled, recoiled,
                                 voices too high to be men.
How hard the tallest kid smacks another in the shoulder, knocks him over,
                                    the cluster of bodies leaving him
behind
and then the doppler of their laughs,   inexhaustible
fierce speech disappearing   white gym shoes scraping
                                  trying on the profane
                                  nonchalant and so intent
to erase themselves as children, surface replacing surface
                                  he catches up rejoins.

But now, back by the engine, in the front yard,
the grass browns in the drought, spidery clusters of weeds
                                and crab grass
                                the only green.

Some seed lands   on the rock,   in the good soil   on the path
the heart   the heart   the fallow heart   the forgotten field

but the mower cancels and evens the misshapen, shriveling lawn.

David Wright

                                        Neighbor
                                        you have watered the lushness
behind your own fence. The look of you with a hand in your pocket.
                                        Neighbor
                                        your newspapers pile
                                        for a week, unread.

Once the place overcomes intent   asphalt and concrete bloom.
                                        The herb garden withers.
A small rabbit stripped the bean plants to stems.
                                        The mottled lettuce makes
                                        one meal, only.

                                Recall
the longing that brought home these small cuttings and placed
                                  them here,
the hand and the tool that mounded the seeds. Now on the days
                                when it rains,
                dirt froths and grass becomes a sponge.
Pull the withered basil. It stains fingertips with scent.
                            Oregano's sharp hearts—
                            place them on the tongue. Swallow
them dry.
Small convert of the summer   despite the steady, fickle sun.
Prolonged liturgy of the hours public work, *ergon*,
                                      public engines of care.

Oh, the hungry belly, the rain, the urge for the anger and surface
                          of a boy's sudden fist,
                                      power
                        we would love without error,
                                        if we could be sure.

three maps
AIMEE BENDER

A not-so-accurate map by memory of the beloved Museum of Jurassic Technology in L.A., subject of Lawrence Weschler's book: <u>Mr. Wilson's Cabinet of Wonder</u>

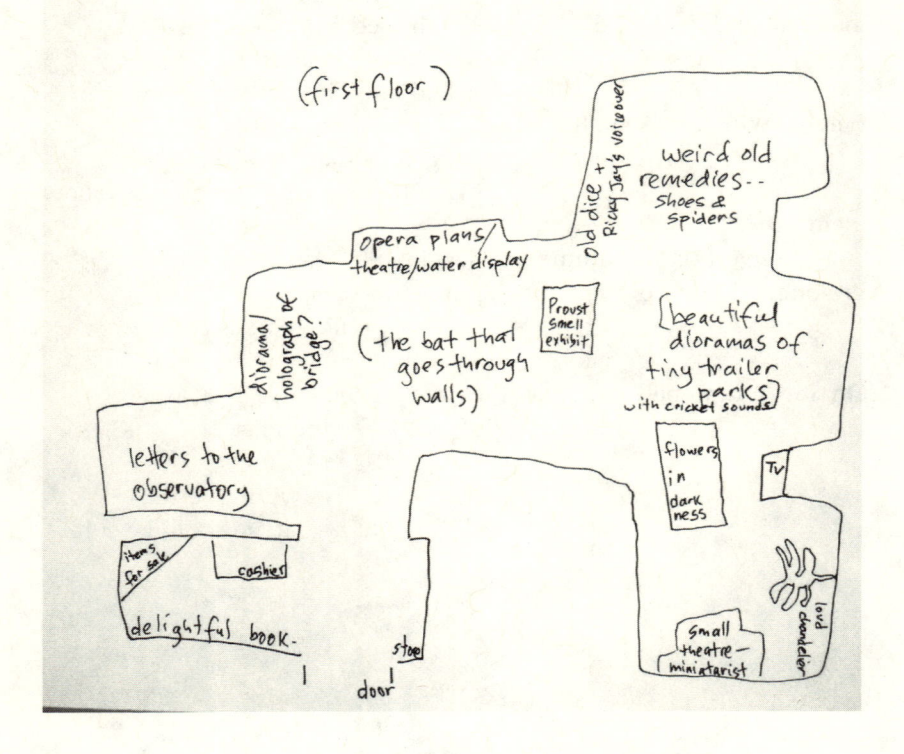

(first floor)

- opera plans/theatre/water display
- old dice + Ricky Jay's voiceover
- weird old remedies -- shoes & spiders
- diorama/holograph of bridge?
- (the bat that goes through walls)
- Proust smell exhibit
- [beautiful dioramas of tiny trailer parks] with cricket sounds
- letters to the observatory
- flowers in darkness
- TV
- items for sale
- cashier
- delightful book
- stop! door
- small theatre—miniaturist
- loud chandelier

Aimee Bender

⁓⁓⁓⁓⁓ = text

This is messy, but it's a fairly accurate map of the path my eye takes as I read a page.

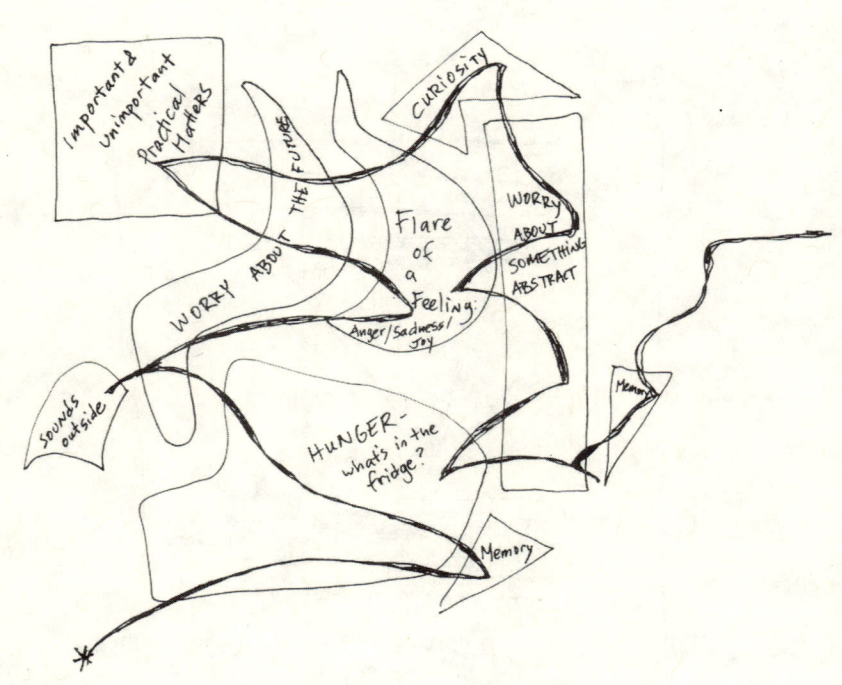

Synapse Map: one minute

Driving I-15
Jill Talbot

I do not want to take back any of the streets I have lost. I do not want to reclaim any cities. I lost Washington Avenue to Hal. A whole town to Shaw. The blue house on Stover Street to Kenny, though maybe I still have the way the morning sun warmed the kitchen. I surrendered Tech Terrace Park to Jason, along with a bar on Nineteenth Street. Brian owns the second story of that stained-glass-windowed restaurant where we shared a salad and too much wine the night before I left town, the night I drove away in my black Jeep, my hand tossed up in a final thank you at the corner of University. For years, I let Mike have the Vegas Strip, though enough years and enough visits back have now rendered it a long avenue of magic, for when my three-year-old sticks her head out the back window in wonder on a desert night, I need no part of what I should have let go of long ago.

I have always let men have cities, streets, and I shouldn't have because they abandoned them long before I did, leaving me to drive through a conversation we once had across from campus, past the porch where we once read Raymond Carver to one another, by an apartment where I used to spend the night, shower. It's been five years, and I'm still not going back to Lubbock, Texas, because I know I'd be going back to Friday afternoons in the Sheraton, a balcony on Fourteenth Street, and a running trail, and I'd worry that Room 236 or the white wooden railing or mile two will not remember me, as if I were never really there, just the shadow that once followed someone she loved. I tried going back to a house across from the Eagle River once, but the shudders of a summer strengthened more than my resolve to say goodbye to it, and I turned my car around before I could even see the street where I once waited for him to come home, when he was still coming home.

Yesterday, I drove the hour and a half to see you. Turned off my cell phone and the Allman Brothers CD and told you stories. There never seems to be enough time to tell you all of me, and I want you to hear: the first time I watched my dad lose a football game, the night I looked downstairs to find my brother open a bottle of wine hours after everyone else had stopped drinking, the way my mother pronounced "I love you" as she left her mother sitting in a yellow chair because she had never given herself permission to walk away without the words, the night Kenny drove twenty-six hours straight because when he called, he heard too long alone, too long drinking in my voice. I kept the cruise at eighty-two and made the winding curves north, talking to a road. Talking to you. I told you of all the streets and towns and corners I surrendered so that you would know I am coming to you without a country. I am drawing you a map of me and of that stretch of highway you've never seen so that it will never be yours, never mine, but ours.

Naturalist's Notes
SARAH REITH

El Cerrito, California

This is a serene, blue-collar neighborhood of thin-walled houses with windows that quiver like wind chimes. Here, the evening haze is sugary and pale. It is several colors at once: spun-candy blue, spiderweb silver, and yellow like the whisper of an old lace ghost. In summertime, it smells of heavy sweating flowers and the slowly melting sea. Because nothing on the water lasts forever, there is a sense in this community of a long, drawn-out grace period, an acknowledgment of intervals.

There are people living here, and little creatures, too. A fat skunk with a frazzled tail lopes hunchbacked past a short thick wall of hedges, then climbs casually onto someone's porch. It stands there blinking underneath the light expectantly, as if it's waiting for someone to open the door, or for a crowd to burst into applause.

The artists here are unassuming, studiously anonymous. Two thick nails drive a Post-it-sized sketch into a phone pole on my street. The picture is quickly drawn, with a sure hand and an eye that seems accurate, though this is hard to say for sure about an illustration of a fluffy Pomeranian revealing several rows of shark teeth. "Biskit, I love you!" reads the caption. It is as calm and absurd as the title of an artwork ought to be. Underneath and to the side of it is a mug shot of a timorously grinning T-Rex. In italics with quotation marks—as if the dinosaur is emphatically saying something, but there is no room for a word balloon—it reads, *"Oh, no, we can't stop here! This is bat country!"*

The third piece isn't quickly drawn, but urgently, as if the artist had a sense of limited time or impending disaster. There is passion and power here, a touching lack of irony. This one is done by the gifted kid, in with the practiced young men.

In efficiently voluptuous lines, like something from an underground tattoo parlor, a naked bald man draws himself into a ball. His face and groin are hidden, but the tension of his limbs is lovingly displayed. He is glued to the gas meter, as if in some obscure act of defiance.

People around here have a broad interpretation of the phone pole as a way to communicate. They don't confine themselves to lost pet fliers or garage sale ads or exhortations to "Lose weight!" and "Earn money from home!" Two blocks from the miniature gallery, there is a large plastic freezer bag nailed to a phone pole. It is partly obscured by a graceful bough of soft green leaves like sweet shy kisses. When I brush this bough aside, as gently as I would a strand of a sleeping infant's hair, I realize that the freezer bag is bulging heavily with partially liquefied dog shit. There is a carefully laminated note inside, too, smudged but legible: PLEASE CLEAN UP AFTER YOUR DOG. Then, with mounting rage, the tidy capitals begin to slant: I'M SICK OF STEAMING PILES OF DOG SHIT EVERY MORNING!!!

Veering unseeingly past all of it is a long-toed trail of bloody footprints, leading from the crossing at Yosemite and Lassen. The story starts between a set of tire marks, with three savage splatters of heavy blood. I can see the fur lines, etched into the ground in vicious silhouette. I can see where the creature gained its feet and then wound hectically along the sidewalks, through the hedges, down San Pablo, towards the sludgy creek beneath the train tracks. The prints are black and faded now, the soggy paws and fat round teardrop splashes. I saw them when the blood was gluey and bright, on the day I stole the shopping cart from Trader Joe's. I thought it was the trail of a dog in heat, but it was another bloody passion.

There is a little hill that oversees the highway and the sunrise and the wetlands, where the loons all dip their bills into the viscous soup. The long white egrets pick their dainty way among the stones and broken bottles and the little big-eyed things that dig into the sludge. The hill is surrounded by an ineffective moat, a continuation of the creek beneath the tracks. There are signs around the water's edge (though none at Lassen and Yosemite) that read: **DANGER. This area is a designated DANGEROUS AREA. Please exercise caution at ALL TIMES**. There is a smell here of well-used city parks; that is to say, of damp earth drying softly in the salt sea air, and eucalyptus buttons, and children with their grubby, eager hands.

Sarah Reith

The eucalyptus, with their silver leaves, are graceful foreigners here, bending nostalgically toward the horizon. Gently, gently, they aspire to the sky. There are foggy days here, when a thin cloud paste spreads itself across the top of the world, and then, when I peer into its muted glare, the tallest eucalyptus look like black-and-white photographs of stunning clarity. They dwarf the ruddy thick-fingered shrubs that thrive here, squatting squinty-eyed and practical, away from the wind to the ground. When they fall, the eucalyptus stretch across the paths in lavish displays of grief. They expose long, pink gaping wounds where they have lost their limbs, and jagged fleshy splinters, all of it terribly sobering, terribly raw.

A hedge with lemons in it grows so square I think it must have been cut from a mold. I picture a crane lowering a giant, four-cornered paper cutter onto the shrub. Do lemons really grow in hedges? Or is this a hedge encircling a lemon tree, wrapped around it closely like a heavy, branchy coat? I reach for one. "Wait," says Tyson, eyeing a car like a seasoned criminal. He doesn't move until it drives away. Then he plunges an arm into the forest and withdraws it, amid the sounds of a terrific struggle. He presents me with a pair of fat, textured lemons, thin-skinned and oddly shaped, as different from each other as a pair of human faces. "That's enough for tonight," he says nervously. From deep inside the hedge, the lemons shine like lamps.

The color inside them is a deep, wet yellow, almost orange, like globules of honey or plasma. Their smell is thick and excessive and intimate. I like to think of them, being pushed out of the earth where people hang up bags of dog shit and their urgent, loving sketches, where little long-toed creatures fight for life and skunks wait on the porch for the sound of applause.

First Light on Corn
David Scott

for Phoebe

Before the light, there is light
bringing out the blue in things.
The ribbons of roads, the pond,
its sister mist rising,
even the oak finds blue enough
to make the blue spruce blush.
The corn at field's edge is last
to get yellowed. Ears rust
inside green husks. The silk
ignites and reaching tendrils
curl into questions as if burned.
Grackles clutter noisy treetops.
Too late, the blue is gone
except for the heron who waits
in the reeds for glints to stride at.
The sun through the pond's mist
dreams clarity, but all is fuzz
of morning, haze of edges and hedges.
No one will believe what happened
as the first distant treetop
caught fire like some celestial accident.
The blue jay squawks about injustice.
The buzzard rides vapors, squints
for the death he knows will come.
You're still asleep, blue eyelids
fluttering dreams to the surface,
breathing the blue air of the house's
back room. When will it end,
this sleep you call waking?
Show me your yellowing hair.

Southern Utah Storms
J. D. Olenslager

Sometimes in the summer, the lightning doesn't arrive until two a.m. The sky is like obsidian, or black marble suddenly hewn down the center. I always think of Michelangelo. The fat, white veins. The air bristling under the action of protons and electrons. It is like a vacuum, and everything is silent.

The storms last an hour, moving slowly, fighting and flashing with the night, the bright-brilliant strikes flaring in my eyes. I watch from the front deck, the glassy shadows and fierce iridescence slashing at each other. I can't stop watching and lean on the rail until the air returns, until the final bolt has vanished back into the black. Then I remember to breathe again.

I am usually alone, thinking about the way life works. But once after the display had ended and I'd turned to leave, I saw my father sitting in our rocker on the far side of the deck, silhouetted against the light. He'd watched the entire time without saying a thing.

Patterned
Caroline Van Hemert

I've been thinking about mathematics lately, wondering if equations can explain the patterns I see around me. Flying over the western border of the Arctic National Wildlife Refuge in a 1974 Cessna, I stare down at the landscape from above. From this angle, tundra looks like an M. C. Escher sketch—angular shapes painted in summer's yellow-greens. The plane banks and I press my face against scratched glass, searching for animals and birds that look like tiny pieces of dust marring a photograph. White blobs on water mean swans; on land, they typically signal the presence of a single snowy owl (at least at this time of year—any sensible polar bear would be far out of sight on the ice floes). Herds of caribou show up as brown spots en masse with occasional glimpses of antlered protrusions. A blurred coffee-colored shock of fur may be a lone musk ox or, less likely, a brown bear.

The first time I flew over this landscape I couldn't tell geese from foxes, confused shape and size and scale. We'd be flying low, and I'd mistake tussocks, ubiquitous lumps of cottongrass, for four-legged mammals. By now, my eyes have learned to associate patterns with creatures, to discern clues from unique form and movement. But I still start in surprise when I see birds from the air, flying alongside the plane or banking beneath its metallic glimmer. I watch the undulating flight carefully, mesmerized by its motion while willing its path to arc away from mine. Birds generally don't get snagged by the props of small planes, as they do in jets, since single-engine bush planes move slowly enough for easy dodging. But the birds seem impossibly close as I watch them pass by my window, wings pumping gracefully alongside our mechanized flight.

I look down and search for designs tumbling past me in miniature. From the air, the perspective offered by distance lends well to the imagination. Like seeing elephants in a pile of cumulus clouds above—our minds always seeking familiar images, instilling order—I watch tundra patterns morph into shapes. Fields of hexagons transform into scowling faces, turn to geometrically winged birds, and then erupt into a tiny city of buildings and cars and infrastructure. Permafrost, the constant layer of ice that lies beneath the tundra, creates this montage; ice wedges intrude into soil, gradually increasing with each cycle of freeze and thaw. In the wake of these frozen blades, honeycombed depressions arise, eventually giving way to thick-lipped ponds and beaded drainage streams.

Another day, thousands of miles and hundreds of days away, I stand under the scorching midday sun in the Namib Desert. A black and white oryx, a striking desert antelope, looks down at me from above, perched on a dune like a four-legged sentinel. I crouch over the ground to examine fine fissures and deep-set gaps in the midst of what used to be a pond. These pans, sucked dry of moisture until next season's rains, form small, ever-shrinking circles of caked mud, laid down among undulating red dunes and fine waves of sand. The sticky pond bottoms, originally saturated with standing water, begin to separate along predictable lines as evaporation leaves a hexagonal web of cracks in its wake.

Across other landscapes, bubbles aggregate into similar hexagonal patterns in seafoam, igneous rock cools into six-sided columns, rivers branch at triple junctions, all following the path of least resistance. In their honeycomb constructions, bees illustrate a model of efficiency that we have since claimed as our own.

Hexagons appear in human biology as universally as they do across nature. Our center of light sensitivity, the path of visual perception itself, sees sunlight refracted through miniature honeycombs. Less than one square millimeter in size, this specialized part of our retina called the fovea functions as a lens of tiny hexagons. We see our surroundings through a mosaic of conical photoreceptors, arranged in tiny, six-sided arrays. Color spots also assemble themselves in hexagonal patterns, and we witness the mark of mathematics painted on the backs of leopards, etched across the flanks of a fawn.

Long before the advent of mathematical software and electron microscopes, hexagons elbowed their angular bodies into art and mythology. They wove their way into Islamic rug designs and dominated ceramic depictions of Mojave archetypes. How could our ancestors have known that from invisible atoms to honeycombed continents to the microscopic anatomy of our eyes, we exist in a six-sided world? Did ancient artists dream hexagons into being or simply mirror what they saw around them, reconstructing nature into art, "coincidence" into meaning? I can no longer see a meandering river without imagining the possibilities of a snowflake, cannot look at roosters through chicken wire absent of leopards' spots. I dream of six-sided leaves and an extra toe. I see hexagons in my freckles, triple junctions in my honeycombs.

In science, we often discover what we seek. Early theories about the alignment of the continents suggested that plates organized themselves according to simple mathematical patterns. Eighteenth-century geologists sketched neat polygons on maps, aligning mountain belts, connecting invisible and unlikely dots as evidence of a contracting or expanding earth. Unable to imagine how mountains and fault lines could be anything *but* patterned, their science reflected a belief in the destiny of numbers. According to contemporary theories of continental drift, these forced attempts at order are easily dismissed as mysticism and numerology. Objectivity has become our divinity—facts, not faith, must dictate scientific theory.

But perched above the earth in a rickety Cessna, I stare out the window at fragments of tundra that refuse to obey six-sidedness and wonder how often patterns reject their bounds. Perhaps the permafrost misbehaved last year, or beaded streams became rivulets. Maybe a slight depression altered the path of the ice, and, hence, changed the shape of the raised soil. Suddenly, a white shape comes into view and I dismiss it for an oddly behaving swan, traveling along the ground with heaving motions. But it doesn't match what I know about swans and I ask the pilot to circle once, then again, and the white speck comes into focus. It rises up on two legs to survey the annoyance flying above, and I nearly shriek. It's a polar bear this time, walking where it shouldn't be, uprooting tussocks in search of ground squirrels and voles. We move away from the bear and I watch it swipe the yellow ground, pawing at polygons and disrupting their borders.

The Archipelago
Evan Morgan Williams

Five hundred miles from the mainland, obscured by the curve of the earth, the islands of a nameless archipelago dot a patch of blue tarpaulin sea. Barren, old, crumbling, the islands are the only defined points on a watery plain that is as vacant and forlorn as sky. Cargo ships chugging across the sea leave wakes of foam, and the wakes crisscross like pick-up sticks, but purposeless currents dissolve these lines. Jet trails across the sky repeat this behavior, the perfect lines, the breaking apart. Clouds of fish drift below, clouds of rain above. Sheens of oil. A stray, melting iceberg from the south. A fishing net torn loose. Nothing holds fast. Not even the islands of the archipelago. They are old and chalky, and they are crumbling into the sea; most have eroded to fewer than a hundred yards wide; the lowest ones are submerged during storms. Someday, the islands of the archipelago will wash away.

The best navigational charts put the number of islands at about two hundred. The shorelines are sheer cliffs, jagged and white as bergs, crowded with puffins, cormorants, and gulls. Every island lies within sight of several others, and no island is separated from another by more than two hops. On a map, if you pinned down segments of string linking the islands, you would describe a network more entwined than the strands of a spider web. But understand this: if you tried to pull the string into a knot, gently, the tangled connections would amount to nothing more than a simple loop. It would be as if the archipelago were not even there.

A long time ago, a people settled the archipelago. Where they originated, why they abandoned their old lives, and where they thought they were going, are not known, but at some time they boarded rafts, drifted across the sea, and washed up on the islands. The people dwelled in caves they carved into the mealy cliffs. Here began a harsh, new way of life. There was no way to leave.

Tourists, mariners, archeologists, and relic hunters have explored the caves and found simple gear for fishing: sinewy nets, fishtraps, crab cages. The caves have yielded ivory knitting needles and spinning bobbins, and even a simple loom strung across four ribs of a bow whale. Evidently, the people gathered flax from a red flower that grows on the rocky humps of the islands, and from this flax they made a variety of fine, strong, scarlet ropes. Samples have been found of twine and string, woven cord, braided ropes, and several gauges of spun thread. The walls of the caves display faded, peeling frescoes, and the frescoes depict men casting fishing lines, women braiding children's hair, instructions for tying dozens of knots, and children swinging from a rope over blue water turned milky from the dissolving cliffs.

The layout of each cave is a marvel, a maze, as intricate as an island can stand without caving in. Maybe in the early days the caves were simple, but to make space for the growing population, they grew more complex: additional wall space for frescoes, twists and turns to confuse intruders. Of course, a resident would have found the passages familiar and comforting; each cave simplifies to a loop. Keep your hand on the left wall as you walk, and trace the frescoes with your fingertips. Do not let go. You will trace the entire cave and return to your starting place.

A few expertly lashed rafts have been found, although there are no trees on the islands. You have to assume that the people kept the best rafts from their flotilla and salvaged boards from the rafts that were no longer serviceable. The frescoes do not show it, but you can imagine the people traveling locally on these rafts, island to island, sharing technology, food, and stories, stitching back and forth like guppies in an aquarium. Of course, the islands in the center of the archipelago would have seen the most traffic, and their frescoes depict people grown fat from puffin eggs, lounging in the sun at the mouth of their caves, lacing string designs between their fat fingers. The people on the peripheral islands may have lived in hunger and desperation and fought among themselves for puffin meat. The frescoes show nothing like that, but of course there would have been no dignity in recording those things.

As much as anyone can determine from the evidence, the people of the archipelago lived meager, primitive lives. Their rafts were flimsy, their fishing gear simple. No weapons, no kitchen utensils (not even a cookfire), no religious artifacts, and no toys have been found. One fresco depicts a storyteller delighting a group of children with a loop of string laced around his fingers in the outline of a seabird—like cat's cradle—but that is all. Only in the making of rope and the tying of knots did the people show any ingenuity. The people appear to have had an advanced understanding of knots. You can infer from the frescoes that knots were their central, organizing device. A midwife ties a knot around an umbilical cord. Children learn a new knot, a new braid, and a new rope trick every year. A set of knots for boys, a set of knots for girls. A priest binds two wrists together during a wedding. A family tugs at a loaf of braided bread. A criminal dangles from a hangman's noose. A crowd lashes rocks to a dead man and heaves his body from a cliff.

As well, samples of knotted rope have been found that are too elaborate to have any practical use, and even suggest advanced mathematical reasoning. The ropes were left in a garbage pile—fish bones, shells, frayed nets—as though the makers did not consider the knots to be worth anything. And it is true: such sophisticated ropework had no application to these people's simple lives. It begs the question, still unanswered: what did the people who left those knots value? What did they not throw away?

Of all the relics that people have found, perhaps the most remarkable are the talking ropes. With scores of knots at their disposal, these people had the makings of an alphabet, the knots functioning like letters of print. Such ropes have been found in some of the caves. The longer ropes may record sagas, the shorter ones proverbs, lists, or data. A rope, dragged across your palm, reads like Braille. Snapped like a lariat, it releases a prayer. Before they knew what they had, a few relic hunters untied some of the ropes, abrogating their stories. Of course, no one can break the code, for it is not alphabetic, but contextual, nuanced. A bowline could stand for strength, a figure-eight knot for a matrix, a square knot for healing. Put those three in order, and so on. That's not enough for a story, but maybe an experienced teller could weave a tale from it. It befalls you only to imagine what these people might have said as they wandered their caves, clambered to the brushy slopes above, cast fishing lines into the sea, and combed, braided, knitted, wove, spun, tied.

On one island, where the cave had collapsed, an archeologist unearthed an especially long talking-rope. From the type of knots, he determined that it had been tied by a teenage boy, and from a kind of periodicity in the patterns, he surmised that it might have been a diary. A lot of speculation has grown around what this boy might have recorded. Maybe one day, the boy practiced a rope trick to impress a girl; another day, he went fishing; or he worried about the tall waves lapping at the entrance to his family's cave; he was hungry and his parents boarded a raft to beg food from another island, but never returned. The final twenty or so knots are looser than the others. Towards the end, they are slack. The last several feet are blank.

Anyone is free to speculate about these things.

The islands being so steep and bare, the people's fascination with knots is not surprising. Knots held things in place, kept supplies from blowing away, kept children from falling over a cliff. Maybe that is what knots symbolized: security, purchase, a hold on reality. On the other hand, maybe the people felt tied to this place unwillingly, bound to this barren, crumbling archipelago, despairing of ever getting away. Maybe the knots were a tether, a leash, a curse.

What happened to these people? How did the culture end? A collapse of the fishery? A storm? A war? A diaspora doomed to fail? There are a thousand theories, but the key, usually ignored, may be a single knot. The frescoes on several of the walls depict a ball of rope, writhing, hopelessly tangled, with a hundred little elbow joints bending this way and that in the mesh. Loose strands protrude in all directions, and at the end of each strand, a small brown hand reaches. The knot's meaning is unclear. It also appears in fishing tackle, in the braids of children's hair, at the tips of lariats, and in fanciful string designs you could lace through your fingers. It could symbolize unity, community, trust, strength, sustenance, pleasure, the circle of life. In this people's language of knots, maybe they spelled the name of God right there in their hands. Why, then, this: with a little coaxing, kneading, and prying, the sacred knot undoes itself. Easy. Let it slip from your fingers, and you are left with an empty loop, the unpronounceable truth.

Here is what some researchers believe. Once per year, a good climber tied a long rope to his waist and spidered across the cliffs. Playing out the rope, the people measured the dwindling circumference of their crumbling island homes. A knot in the rope marked the annual erosion. Every year, as the rope shortened, the people saw what was happening, and they decided to leave before the islands completely dissolved. They undid everything they had done there. They weren't tied to this place at all.

They crowded onto the last of their rafts, lashed their few possessions, and floated away. Maybe a few rafts made it to the edges of the archipelago, caught the ocean current, and broke free. Who knows where those people ended up? The rest of the rafts drifted from island to island, powerless to escape the narrow straits, the confining waters, the net of islands. A raft would squeeze between two islands toward a promising gap of blue sea, but another chalky bluff would loom in its path. Again and again, the currents guided the rafts teasingly to the edge of the archipelago, then back to the familiar center. The routes of the rafts intertwined in a knot, increasingly and desperately tangled. Eventually the people depleted their supplies and accepted whatever island the waves marooned their raft upon. They would never leave.

The tangled, sacred knot took its final, perfect, bewildering form.

notes on contributors

JULIANNA BAGGOTT'S fourth novel is *Which Brings Me to You* (co-written with Steve Almond). Her second book of poems, *Lizzie Borden in Love*, was published in September. She also writes a series of novels for younger readers, *The Anybodies* (now in development with Nickelodeon Movies at Paramount) under the pen name N. E. Bode. She teaches at Florida State University's Creative Writing Program.

REBECCA BARRY'S fiction has appeared in *Ploughshares, Tin House, Mid-American Review, One Story,* and *Best New American Voices 2005*. She was short-listed in *Best American Short Stories 2000* and *Best American Short Stories 2004* and her nonfiction has appeared in many publications, including *The Washington Post Magazine, The New York Times Magazine,* and *Best American Travel Writing 2003*. Her collection of short stories, including "Eye. Arm. Leg. Heart." will be published by Simon and Schuster in 2007. She lives in Trumansburg, New York.

AIMEE BENDER is the author of the short story collections *Willful Creatures* and *The Girl in the Flammable Skirt* and the novel *An Invisible Sign of My Own*. Her stories have appeared in *Granta, GQ, Harper's, The Paris Review,* and other magazines and have been heard on PRI's *This American Life*. She teaches at the University of Southern California.

SARAH BLACKMAN is an MFA candidate at the University of Alabama, where she served as the fiction editor for *Black Warrior Review*. Her work has most recently appeared in *Best New American Voices 2006, The Laurel Review, Parthenon West,* and *The Greensboro Review*.

MICHAEL P. BRANCH is a Virginian who lives in the remote high desert of the western Great Basin in Nevada, where he writes, plays blues, and curses at baseball on the radio. He has published five books and more than one hundred essays and reviews, including essays in *The Utne Reader, Orion,* and *Isotope*. He teaches in the graduate program in Literature and Environment at the University of Nevada Reno, and his most recent book is *Reading the Roots: American Nature Writing before Walden* (University of Georgia Press, 2004).

Brian Doyle is the editor of *Portland Magazine* at the University of Portland. His essays have appeared in the *Best American Essays* collections of 1998, 1999, 2003, and 2005, and he is the author of seven books, most recently *The Wet Engine* (about the muddle and mangle and music and miracle of hearts) and *The Grail* (in which a total wine doofus spends a very cheerful year indeed in an Oregon pinot noir vineyard).

Katie Fallon teaches creative writing at Virginia Tech. Her creative nonfiction has appeared in *Fourth Genre, River Teeth, Appalachian Heritage*, and elsewhere.

Gary Fincke's fourth collection of stories, *Sorry I Worried You* (University of Georgia Press, 2004), won the Flannery O'Connor Award for Short Fiction, and Michigan State published *Amp'd: A Father's Backstage Pass*, his nonfiction account of his son's life in two signed rock bands, in 2004. His latest book is a collection of poems, *Standing around the Heart* (University of Arkansas Press, 2005). He directs the Writers Institute at Susquehanna University.

Christien Gholson's poems and stories have appeared or will appear in *Hanging Loose, Mudlark, Big Bridge, 2River, Cimarron Review, Lilliput Review,* and *Alaska Quarterly Review,* among others. A book of linked prose poems, *On the Side of the Crow,* was recently published by Hanging Loose Press. He lives in New Mexico.

Sarah Gorham is the author of three collections of poetry: *The Cure, The Tension Zone,* and *Don't Go Back to Sleep*. She coedited with Jeffrey Skinner the anthology *Last Call: Poems on Alcoholism, Addiction, and Deliverance*, published in 1997 by Sarabande Books. Recent poems and essays have appeared in *American Poetry Review, Southern Review, Five Points, Virginia Quarterly Review, Gettysburg Review, Fourth Genre, Prairie Schooner,* and *Poets and Writers*. Gorham serves as president and editor-in-chief of Sarabande Books, an independent literary press.

Seth Harwood's fiction has been published in *Twenty Pounds of Headlights, Inkwell,* and *Post Road,* among others. He is a graduate of the Iowa Writers' Workshop and lives in Berkeley, California, with his wife, Joelle, and their dog Hadley. For more information and to listen to his podcast novel, visit www.sethharwood.com.

NOTES ON CONTRIBUTORS

PETER MAKUCK'S stories, essays, poems, and reviews have appeared in *The Hudson Review, Poetry,* and *The Sewanee Review.* Author of five volumes of poems, he has edited *Tar River Poetry* at East Carolina University for twenty-seven years. *Off Season in the Promised Land,* a new volume of poems, was published by BOA Editions Ltd. in October 2005. His short story collection, *Costly Habits* (University of Missouri Press, 2002), was nominated for a Pen/Faulkner Award. He lives with his wife, Phyllis, on Bogue Banks, one of North Carolina's barrier islands.

JILL MCCORKLE is the author of five novels: *The Cheer Leader, July 7th, Tending to Virginia, Ferris Beach* and *Carolina Moon,* and three story collections, most recently *Creatures of Habit.* Her work has appeared in *The Atlantic, Ploughshares, Best American Short Stories* and *New Stories from the South,* among other publications. The recipient of the New England Book Award, the John Dos Passos Prize, and the North Carolina Award for Literature, she has taught creative writing at UNC-Chapel Hill, Tufts, Harvard, Brandeis and Bennington College. She is currently on faculty at North Carolina State University as the Lee Smith Writer in Residence.

CLAUDIA MONPERE'S poetry and fiction has appeared in *The Kenyon Review, Prairie Schooner, The Spoon River Poetry Review, Puerto del Sol, Calyx,* and elsewhere. She is a recipient of the Georgetown Review Fiction Award, and her essays appear in collections by Persea Books and the Haworth Press. She directs the Creative Writing Program at Santa Clara University.

ALISSA NUTTING'S work is recently published in *Playgirl* and forthcoming in *Swink Magazine.* She is an MFA candidate at the University of Alabama, where she is managing editor for *Black Warrior Review* and assistant editor for *Fairy Tale Review* and *Alabama Heritage Magazine.*

J. D. OLENSLAGER is currently an English student at Southern Utah University. While he has published numerous poems in local magazines, this is his first publication outside of Utah. He is planning on moving to the East coast for graduate school in the fall.

PATRICK PHILLIPS'S first book, *Chattahoochee,* recieved the 2005 Kate Tufts Discovery Award as well as a "Discovery"/The Nation Award. Poems from the collection have appeared in many magazines, including *Poetry, Ploughshares,* and the *Virginia Quarterly Review.* He recently completed a doctorate in renaissance literature at New York University.

LIA PURPURA'S new book of essays, *On Looking,* was published in August 2006 by Sarabande Press. New poems and essays are forthcoming in *Agni Review, Tin House, Sonora Review,* and *DoubleTake.* She is writer-in-residence at Loyola College in Baltimore, Maryland.

SARAH REITH completed her BA in English at Mills College in Oakland, California. She is now working on her MA in German literature at San Francisco State University. Her work has appeared in *The Village Rambler, R-K-V-R-Y, The Hurricane Review,* and *Poetry Motel.* Originally from San Francisco, she lives now in El Cerrito, with a view of the Golden Gate Bridge.

ALICITA RODRIGUEZ lives in a Colorado ghost town with her boyfriend and their three crazy dogs. She teaches at Western State College. Her work has appeared or is forthcoming in *TriQuarterly, New Letters,* and *Fiction International.*

REG SANER'S latest nonfiction book is *The Dawn Collector.* His poetry collections include *So This Is the Map* and *Climbing into the Roots,* the latter the winner of the first Walt Whitman prize for poetry. For more information on Reg Saner, see page fifty-five.

DAVID G. W. SCOTT'S poems have appeared in numerous literary publications, including *Poet Lore, Euphony, The Madison Review, West Branch, New Delta Review, The Lyric, The Greensboro Review, Red White and Blues* (University of Iowa Press), and an essay is forthcoming in *About What Was Lost* (Plume, 2006). Winner of the Irene Leache Foundation's award in free verse poetry, he is also a recipient of fellowships in fiction and poetry from the Delaware Division of the Arts. He received a PEN Discovery Award for Fiction in 2004.

NOTES ON CONTRIBUTORS

ROBERT ANTHONY SIEGEL'S second novel, *All Will Be Revealed*, is forthcoming from MacAdam/Cage. His first novel was *All the Money in the World*. He teaches creative writing at the University of North Carolina Wilmington.

ABRAHAM SMITH hails from Ladysmith, Wisconsin. His recent poems have appeared or are forthcoming in *jubilat, Northwest Review, Denver Quarterly,* and *Court Green*. He was a 2004–05 Writing Fellow at the Fine Arts Work Center, Provincetown, Massachusetts.

JOAN SNYDER'S work has appeared in many public collections, including the Museum of Modern Art, the Metropolitain Musuem of Art, and the Whitney Museum of American Art. For more information on Joan Snyder, see page sixty-eight.

JILL TALBOT has published in Under the Sun, Cimarron Review, and Blue Mesa Review, among others. She is the co-editor of The Art of Friction: Where (Non)Fictions Come Together (University of Texas Press, 2008), an anthology that explores the fiction/nonfiction debate. Her first memoir, Loaded, will be published by Seal Press in 2007. She lives in Boise, Idaho.

CAROLINE VAN HEMERT currently works as a wildlife biologist, and recently received her MA in creative writing. Much of her time is spent pursuing field studies across Alaska, Botswana, and other remote parts of the globe—chasing birds, charging through brush, and attempting to make sense of the data that result.

EVAN MORGAN WILLIAMS has published over thirty short stories in magazines including *Alaska Quarterly Review, Northwest Revew,* and *Blue Mesa Review*. He has stories current or forthcoming in *Alimentum, The Fourth River, The Healing Muse,* and *You Are Here*. His website is www.pahoehoe.edublogs.org.

DAVID WRIGHT'S poems have appeared in *Artful Dodge, The Mars Hill Review, The MacGuffin,* and many others. His most recent poetry collection is *A Liturgy for Stones* (Cascadia, 2003). A past recipient of an Illinois Arts Council fellowship for poetry, Wright lives in central Illinois with his family.

Ecotone welcomes unsolicited works of creative nonfiction, fiction, and poetry with a specific focus on place. Submissions are accepted between August 15 and April 30 only.

Mail one prose piece and/or one to six poems at a time (mail genres separately). Prose should be typed double-spaced on one side of the page and be no longer than ten thousand words. Please query before submitting anything longer. Poems should be typed either single- or double-spaced on one side of the page. We have no preference in regards to names in headers or footers, or to staples or paper clips. Novel and memoir excerpts are acceptable if they are self-contained.

Please do not send multiple submissions in the same genre, and do not send another manuscript until you hear about the first. Include your full name and address on all envelopes. In general, address submissions to the editor in your genre. We generally follow the *Chicago Manual of Style*.

All manuscripts and correspondence regarding submissions should be accompanied by a self-addressed, stamped envelope (S.A.S.E.) for a response; no replies will be given by e-mail. Expect three months for a decision. We do not print previously published work, and we do not accept simultaneous submissions. We assume no responsibility for delay, loss, or damage. For more information about literary magazines, consult directories such as *NewPages*, *The Writer's Market,* and *The International Directory of Literary Magazines and Small Presses*.

Mail submissions to:
Ecotone
Genre Editor
Department of Creative Writing
University of North Carolina Wilmington
601 South College Road
Wilmington, NC 28403-3297

Ecotone does not accept electronic submissions.

Visit us online at www.uncw.edu/ecotone.

EVENT™
new & established writers

Creative Non-Fiction Contest

$1,500

Three winners will each receive $500 plus payment for publication in *Event* 36/3. Other manuscripts may be published.

Final Judge: TBA. Myrna Kostash, Andreas Schroeder, Sharon Butala, Tom Wayman, Di Brandt, Terry Glavin, Karen Connelly and Charles Montgomery are just some of our past judges.

Writers are invited to submit manuscripts exploring the creative non-fiction form. Check your library for back issues of *Event* with previous winning entries and judges' comments. Contest back issues are available from *Event* for $7.49 (includes GST and postage; US$7 for American residents; CAN$12 for overseas residents).

Note: Previously published material, or material accepted elsewhere for publication, cannot be considered. Maximum entry length is 5000 words, typed, double-spaced. The writer should not be identified on the entry. Include a separate cover sheet with the writer's name, address, phone number / email, and the title(s) of the story (stories) enclosed. Include a SASE (Canadian postage / IRCs / US$1). Douglas College employees are not eligible to enter.

Entry Fee: Multiple entries are allowed, however, *each* entry must be accompanied by a $29.95 entry fee (includes GST and a one-year subscription; make cheque or international money order payable to *Event*). Those already subscribing will receive a one-year extension. American and overseas entrants please pay in US dollars.

Deadline for Entries: Postmarked by April 16, 2007.

EVENT™ P.O. Box 2503, New Westminster, BC
Canada V3L 5B2
Phone: (604) 527-5293   Fax: (604) 527-5095
e-mail: event@douglas.bc.ca

Douglas College

Visit our website at **http://event.douglas.bc.ca**

fiction   chapbook
    comics
black   review
    poetry
        nonfiction
    art
        warrior

Suscriptions: Submissions: Web:
One issue $10   BWR   webdelsol.com/bwr
One year $16   Box 862936   bwr@ua.edu
                       Tuscaloosa, AL 35486

B(W)R
BLACK WARRIOR REVIEW

PRAISE FOR post road

"*Post Road*, from its inception, has been an exotic and intelligent literary treat. I always like to see what they come up with each issue, and they never fail to surprise, entertain, and enlighten."

JONATHAN AMES

"I always read *Post Road* with great enthusiasm. In its stealthy, unassuming way, it has become one of the most reliable and ambitious literary magazines in America."

RICK MOODY

"*Post Road* is one of the most interesting and exciting literary magazines out there. If you care about reading and writing, do yourself a favor and check it out."

TOM PERROTTA

"*Post Road* maps the way to the freshest and funkiest literary territories. As the group The Postal Service does for music, *Post Road* fuses eclectic elements into something whole and wholly new."

ELIZABETH SEARLE

"The editors' enthusiasm is palpable; they consistently provide a lively home for writing worth reading."

AMY HEMPEL

"Post Road has the goods. I not only fall on them and read them like hot news when they come in the door, I keep them lined up on my shelf like little books, because that's what they are."

JONATHAM LETHEM

1 YEAR: $18, 2 YEARS: $34   WWW.POSTROADMAG.COM

ARTCRITICISMFICTIONNONFICTIONPOETRYTHEATREETCETERARECOMMENDATIONS

THE JOURNAL
writing this good doesn't need a fancy name

the journal short story prize
1st prize $1000 and story publication
deadline may 1

william allen creative nonfiction prize
1st prize $500 and essay publication
deadline january 15

the osu press/the journal prize in poetry
1st prize $3000 and book publication
september postmark

the ohio state university prize in short fiction
1st prize $1500 and book publication
november postmark

for submission, subscription, contest, and donation information:
http://english.osu.edu/journals/the_journal/

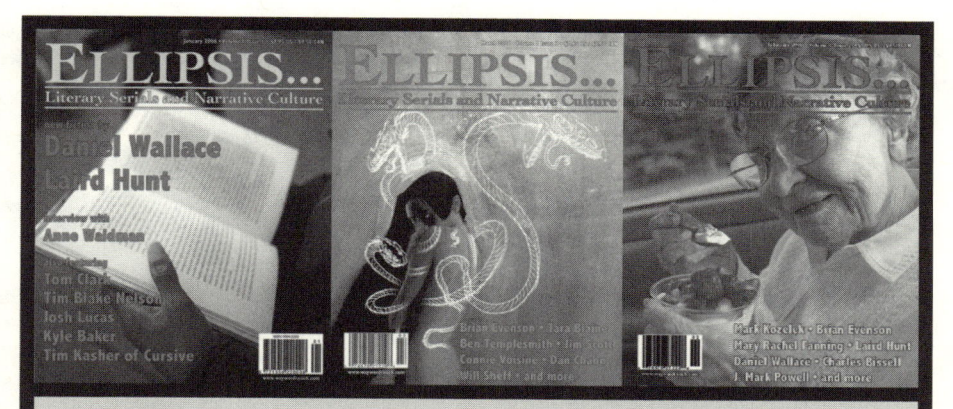

ELLIPSIS...
Literary Serials and Narrative Culture

On newsstands monthly

- Serial fiction
- Poetry
- Short Stories
- Interviews and articles

For News • Subscriptions • Submissions

www.waywardcouch.com

MAR
Mid-American Review

www.bgsu.edu/midamericanreview

Poetry
Fiction
Nonfiction
Translations
Interviews
Reviews

**Host a literary gathering in your home
four times a year—
only $24, and you don't have to clean up!**

Settle into a comfortable chair with your favorite beverage and the latest issue of *The Georgia Review*.

Go mind to mind with essayists such as William H. Gass, Edward Hirsch, Mary T. Lane, Barry Lopez, and Liza Wieland.

Savor similes and stanzas from a wide range of poets: Rita Dove, Stephen Dunn, Alice Friman, Bob Hicok, Jane Hirshfield, Garrett Hongo, Philip Levine, Pattiann Rogers, Dave Smith, and others.

Enter new fictional realities with Sarah Shun-lien Bynum, Ewing Campbell, Janice Daugharty, Alice Fulton, Bret Lott, Joyce Carol Oates, George Singleton, Liza Ward and others.

Delight and challenge your senses with a wide array of visual art, usually in full color.

Discover recent books in essay-reviews by Jeff Gundy, Judith Kitchen, Kathleen Snodgrass, and others.

Just $24—that's only $6 per issue. Cheaper than a movie ticket, and maybe cheaper than the popcorn, but lasts much longer.

THE GEORGIA REVIEW
012 Gilbert Hall, The University of Georgia, Athens, GA 30602-9009

Enjoy excerpts and secure ordering online at
www.uga.edu/garev
or call our office toll-free at **(800) 542-3481**.

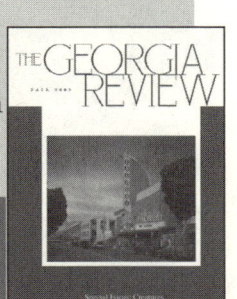

Western State College of Colorado's
Marginalia
literary magazine

Publishes yearly in the fall
Issues available for $9 each
Accepts online submissions only
Reads all year
Sponsors an annual college prose contest

At Marginalia, we are interested in the interplay between the contained text and its surrounding negative space. For this reason, we encourage work that demonstrates mastery of any given genre, as well as work that transgresses or blurs established forms.

Authors we've published:
Mary Crow,
Brian Evenson,
R.S. Gwynn,
Laird Hunt,
Mark Irwin,
Steve Katz,
Gina Ochsner,
George Saunders,
George Singleton,
Wendy Walker

Complete submissions and contest guidelines, and sample work available at
www.western.edu/marginalia

reDiViDer

a journal of new literature

Redivider, a journal of new literature and art, is run by the graduate students of the Writing, Literature, and Publishing Department at Emerson College in Boston. Published twice yearly, *Redivider* features poetry, fiction, creative non-fiction, plays and art by, as well as interviews with and reviews of, established and emerging writers and artists from around the world.

Darkly comic yet cuttingly sad, accessible yet challenging, *Redivider* aims to be as intriguing, offbeat, and compulsively readable as the personal ads. Intelligent and eclectic, our writers take risks. Unlike some other journals whose pieces seem to blur into a unified monotone, our magazine is polyvocal and compelling, so much so that we bet you'll read each issue cover to cover!

To subscribe, mail this form and your check or money order to:

Redivider
Attn: Subscriptions
Emerson College
120 Boylston Street
Boston, MA 02116

_____ One-Year Subscription (two issues): $10.00
_____ Two-Year Subscription (four issues): $18.00
_____ Sample Issue: $6.00
_____ Back Issue: $6.00, or $10.00 for Spring 2004, special double issue
         Please specify back issue_____

Name _____
Address _____
_____
City _____ State _____ Zip _____
Email Address (Optional) _____

Questions? Check out our website at http://pages.emerson.edu/publications/redivider or email us at redivider_editor@yahoo.com.

UNCW *Creative Writing*

MFA in Fiction Poetry Creative Nonfiction

JOIN US in one of the **few independent creative writing departments** in the nation and study writing in workshops, craft seminars, and individual conferences with our distinguished faculty. Participate in **The Publishing Laboratory**, a fully functioning micropress, or work on *Ecotone*, our national literary magazine of environmental writing. All within a welcoming coastal community rich in culture, natural history, heritage, and support for the arts.

Teaching assistantships, fellowships, and scholarships are available.

Faculty Lavonne Adams, Tim Bass, Barbara Brannon, Wendy Brenner, Mark Cox, Clyde Edgerton, Philip Furia, Philip Gerard, David Gessner, Rebecca Lee, Sarah Messer, Malena Mörling, Robert Siegel, Michael White

Visiting Faculty Recent guests include Rick Bass, Richard Bausch, Robert Creeley, Mark Doty, Allan Gurganus, Brenda Hillman, Randall Kenan, Philip Levine, Alison Lurie, Jill McCorkle, Heather McHugh, Donna Tartt, Terry Tempest Williams

910.962.3070 • mfa@uncw.edu
www.uncw.edu/writers

University of North Carolina **Wilmington**
Department of Creative Writing
601 South College Road, Wilmington NC 28403-5938
UNCW is an EEO/AA institution.

UNCW
CREATIVE WRITING

Innovative programs for writers on the Carolina Coast

ECOTONE
reimagining place

Subscriptions:
Back issues: $5
One-year (two issues): $15
Two-years (four issues): $25
Three-years (six issues): $35

— — — — — — — — —

❐ send me a ___ -year subscription for $___.

Name: _____
Address: _____
_____
Phone number: _____
E-mail address: _____

Mail check payable to UNCW Creative Writing Department, subject line *Ecotone* subscription, and mail to :

Ecotone
Department of Creative Writing
University of North Carolina Wilmington
601 South College Road
Wilmington, NC 28403-3297

ECOTONE
reimagining place

Volume I, Number 1
Winter/Spring 2005

featuring the work of *Mark Doty, Clyde Edgerton, Alicia Erian, Brad Land, Philip Levine, Bill Roorbach, Reg Saner, and Ann Zwinger.*

Volume I, Number 2
Winter/Spring 2006

featuring the work of *Ann Darby, Barbara Fisher, Sheila Kohler, Sebastian Matthews, David Rivard, Jennifer Sinor, and Mike White*